KS1

P1 to 3

E

NS

AUTHOR
Stuart Ball

EDITOR
Gina Walker

ASSISTANT EDITOR
David Sandford

SERIES DESIGNER
Anna Oliwa

DESIGNER
Anna Oliwa

ILLUSTRATIONS
Fred Pipes

COVER ARTWORK
Ian Murray

Text © 2000 Stuart Ball
© 2000 Scholastic Ltd

Designed using Adobe Pagemaker
Published by Scholastic Ltd, Villiers House, Clarendon
Avenue, Leamington Spa, Warwickshire CV32 5PR
Printed by Bell & Bain Ltd, Glasgow

234567890   123456789

British Library Cataloguing-in-Publication Data
A catalogue record for this book is available from the
British Library.

ISBN 0-439-01672-X

Contents

Introduction

Primary science has held its core subject status for over ten years, emphasizing its importance as a vital part of children's education. During this time, the skills and processes that scientists use in their everyday lives have found their way into the primary classroom. The evolution of science investigations began in the early days of the National Curriculum, where perhaps it was felt that the skills of investigation would be adequately addressed within coverage of the 15 Attainment Targets. The revision of the curriculum in 1995 reduced the number of Attainment Targets to four, and presented the primary teacher with two programmes of study that provided the basis for scientific investigation: 'Experimental and Investigative Science', or Sc1, and the 'Key Stage Programme of Study', or Sc0. The latest revision of the National Curriculum combines these two areas into one Programme of Study called 'Scientific Enquiry', which could perhaps be seen as the 'essence' of science. It requires far more than just investigative activities in the classroom: it also asks children to consider the safety aspects of their work, the ways in which their work relates to everyday life and how it can help answer questions based on their own ideas.

Children are naturally inquisitive and have an in-built desire to make sense of the world around them. This has been clearly documented by the Nuffield SPACE (Science Processes and Concept Exploration) Project (1990). It shows that children readily create their own perceptions and explanations of the world around them. If we base our science teaching simply on the delivery of facts and knowledge, we develop a science curriculum devoid of rich learning opportunities, as we do not challenge children's preconceptions, which are often misinterpretations. Offering children the opportunity to 'discover' concepts, and thereby challenge their own existing ideas, can help to develop more active and receptive learners. Children who are encouraged to question, use their investigative skills and draw upon their existing knowledge to try to explain their observations can develop a self-motivating desire to learn.

So many investigations in the primary classroom, however, are notoriously flawed – too simple or too complicated in their learning outcome. Many teachers feel that children must 'discover' the 'correct' answer. Some may even tell children the outcome – 'When you exercise your heart beats faster because…' – and then ask children to carry out an investigation to find this out. Why not just carry out the investigation and let children observe this for themselves?

Using an investigative approach to deliver science concepts and knowledge requires a little more time to organize than the straightforward 'delivery of facts' approach, and teachers need to have a clear understanding of the learning objectives involved. But with such an understanding, teachers can focus on specific skills for specific children, develop numeracy and literacy skills and develop the use of ICT, all through a well-planned science investigation.

The AKSIS Project (Association for Science Education and Kings College Science Investigation Study, 1999) has shown that the 'fair test' type of investigation tends to dominate the investigative activities in the primary classroom. However, there are a variety of investigative approaches to science: Fair testing, Identifying and classifying, Pattern seeking, Exploring, Investigating models and Making things. Using a variety of approaches allows children of all abilities to develop their investigative skills and contribute to their own development in science.

The activities in this book provide the classroom teacher with a means by which to carry out and develop his or her own investigations. They attempt to address the areas teachers may find problematic, such as organization, background science knowledge and how to develop activities that are stimulating yet provide valuable learning experiences.

ICT IN SCIENCE

Work in science investigations can be enhanced through the use of ICT, but only if the computer is seen as a tool with which children can interact, rather than as a resource to be used in a passive way. Outlined below are some ways in which the various aspects of ICT can be used as part of the science learning in the primary classroom.

WORD PROCESSORS

A word processor can be used to produce a report of a science investigation. But this can be a lengthy process, as children are rarely speedy typists and simply copying up a report is perhaps the ICT equivalent of colouring in! Word processors in science are best used to produce short direct statements from children about their findings, to be printed out. They are also needed when children are collecting reference materials, and cutting and pasting information from a CD-ROM or a web site. Word-processors are extremely useful when a science report is to be presented in a different way: as a newspaper article, for example, or as a collaborative report. Here children can work as group, contributing their thoughts and ideas. This approach can be made more effective if an adult is available to type the comments made. Word processors can also be great motivators, enabling children who have difficulties with writing to express their ideas clearly, by helping them with spelling and presentation.

GRAPHING PROGRAMS

A graphing program simply draws graphs: children can enter their results into a table and produce the graph of their choice, depending on the program. By producing a simple bar graph, children instantly have a visual representation of any values collected from their investigations. This allows younger children to make comparisons between values, and provides a means by which they can begin to analyse data and draw conclusions. This is important, as young children often do not have the co-ordination skills to draw effective graphs by hand, so the computer enables them to build up experience of working with graphs in science that would otherwise not be available.

CD-ROMs IN SCIENCE

Children can use CD-ROMs to research information. Using a CD-ROM to answer questions that they have created themselves offers children a focus to their activity. Young children can be shown how to use the cut-and-paste facilities to select relevant information for use in their own reports or simply to print out. Many CD-ROM titles have animations and video footage, which can be used as demonstrations, and can make a valuable contribution to children's understanding of science.

MODELLING IN SCIENCE

Modelling programs allow children to explore and interact with a world that exists 'inside' the computer. For example, CD-ROMs are available that allow children to explore the seashore, a rainforest or the inside of the human body. The level of interactivity depends on the software used. Animation and video footage provide simple models and are common in CD-ROM software. Other products, such as My World, enable children to build 'worlds' for themselves. (My World is a series of programs that allows children to use pictures, sound and text to develop and extend learning in a variety of situations. It is available for Windows and Acorn computers from most educational software suppliers.) Adventure programs allow children to explore a variety of 'worlds', solving puzzles in a game-style context.

THE INTERNET

The Internet gives opportunities to access a seemingly limitless source of information. By 'bookmarking' favourite sites, children can quickly find the information they want: the latest weather reports with satellite images, for example, or up-to-date images from the latest Mars mission. Children need a focus and purpose for their use of the Internet, to avoid aimless and time-consuming searching.

The flow of information on the Internet is a two-way process – not only can children access information, but they can also contribute to it. They may be able to present their investigation findings on the school web site, or exchange scientific data with other schools using e-mail.

ASSESSMENT

Before any of the activities in this book are undertaken it is useful to think about the assessment opportunities they can provide. How they are used, and what they are used to assess, very much depends on the learning outcomes that have been decided upon for the lesson. For example, the teacher may wish to assess children on their planning skills. If so, an activity should be chosen that involves fair testing or pattern seeking, and just the parts involving planning and identifying variables should be carried out. If the teacher needs to assess only the children's ability to analyse data and draw conclusions, then the planning and carrying out of the investigation could be done as a demonstration for the whole class, with children working on an individual basis to analyse the results and record their own ideas.

In assessment, we need to know where children are starting from, so that we know where we want to take them. There are a number of useful strategies that we can employ to highlight children's ideas about scientific concepts. When starting new concepts, the teacher should ask the children to record what they already know. For example, children could be asked to draw what the inside the body looks like, showing where the organs are and what they are called. After a teaching input, in which these drawings can be used for discussion, children could draw the inside of the body again and make comments about what they have learned. In investigations, children need to predict and guess outcomes, which provides an ideal opportunity for the teacher to obtain information that can be used for assessment. But to do this effectively, children must be working in an environment that values such an approach and is not overly concerned with obtaining the 'correct' answer. Working in such an environment allows children to feel comfortable about contributing their ideas, makes them more open to other points of view and makes them therefore more receptive to learning.

An extension of such an approach is to use 'concept maps'. Here, children record the words and ideas that they feel are linked to a concept. They then make connections between these words and ideas. The children can be asked to produce maps before and after an investigation or unit of work. These can be compared and differences highlighted, showing how their thinking has changed.

Questioning is an extremely useful tool for assessment, and when it is used to engage children in conversation about their work, deep insights can be made into their scientific thinking.

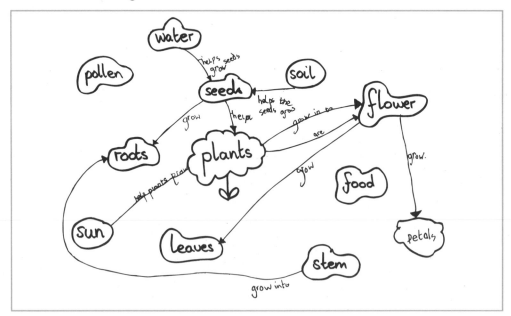

CROSS-CURRICULAR LINKS

Science investigations also provide useful opportunities to assess other aspects of the curriculum, in particular literacy, numeracy and ICT. By focusing on how children research and present their investigations and write their reports, links can be made to work in literacy. Assessment opportunities for numeracy are provided when children produce graphs, analyse data and use measuring equipment. Work with word processors and CD-ROMs can be used to assess ICT, as well as science.

In the activities described in this book, further specific links to other areas of the curriculum can be made through the 'Now or later' sections. For example, there are suggestions of how to extend activities by writing poems, making posters, going on visits to leisure centres and swimming pools, using sound recording software, designing a garden, linking with other schools via e-mail, making models, investigating road safety materials, making a dictionary of science words, creating characters and acting out stories, and so on – all of which have clear connections with other curriculum subjects.

USEFUL READING

Making Sense of Primary Science Investigations, A. Goldsworthy and R. Feasey, rev. S. Ball (ASE, 1997. ISBN 086357 2820)
ASE Guide to Primary Science Education, ed. R. Sherrington (ASE, 1998. ISBN 086357 2901)

Section 1

LIFE PROCESSES AND LIVING THINGS

This section relates to the Programme of Study: Life processes and living things (Sc2). Here children begin to develop the skills they need to ask questions, observe and explore ideas about themselves, animals and plants. Investigations allow children to collect evidence to help them answer questions, while promoting an ethos for the care of living things, the environment and their own health. The very nature of living things in the classroom can make investigations problematic, but the ideas that follow in this section suggest how good science work can be achieved. Throughout, children should be encouraged to use reference materials to find out more about scientific ideas, and to share their ideas through appropriate scientific language, drawings, charts and tables.

HANDY HANDS

RESOURCES AND CLASSROOM ORGANIZATION

The beginning of this investigation involves lots of discussion that could take place during time in the sitting area of the classroom. The investigation could take place over a number of days, with a different part of the activity being undertaken each day.

Each group will need:
■ 'Handy hands' planning and recording sheets – photocopiable page 17
■ several small items of about the same size, such as maths blocks or cubes (or alternatively beads, plastic coins, counters or buttons)
■ a container in which to place the blocks (or other items)
■ drawing paper.

BACKGROUND KNOWLEDGE

Children often think that there is a continuous relationship between a person's age and how big he or she is. It is not always obvious to them that if this were the case, people in their eighties would be very tall indeed! But to young children, people who are older are taller, so this belief is based on their observations. Humans grow rapidly in their early years, then this rate gradually slows, and stops at around twenty.

WHAT TO DO

In order to allow a clear pattern to develop in the results of this investigation, select older children and adults to include in the test.

The activity begins with a great deal of discussion with the class. Discuss what jobs hands can do. Write the children's suggestions down. Children might find it easier to think about the jobs in terms of 'kind or useful things hands do' and 'not so kind or useful things hands do'. They could make lists of their ideas under each of these headings.

Ask the class to think about and to identify all the different parts of the hand. They can do this by looking at their own hands. Ask them to compare their hands with those of other people. Do they notice any differences? Are there any differences between their own hands and the hands of older people?

OBJECTIVES
To give opportunities for children to:
■ understand the importance of collecting evidence when trying to answer a question
■ ask questions
■ make a record of simple observations, comparisons and measurements
■ make simple comparisons and identify simple patterns.

VOCABULARY
Blocks, compare, fingers, grab, hands, hold, measure, palm.

Ask the children which person in the school they think could pick up the biggest number of blocks (or other small items) with one hand. Discuss with the class what factors might affect somebody's ability to pick up blocks, for example, size of hand or length of fingers.

Explain to the children that they are going to draw around their own hands on the 'Handy hands' planning and recording sheet (photocopiable page 17). The sheet asks them to make a simple prediction of how many blocks they think they (or the person they are testing) can hold in one hand. They then need to put a hand into the container of blocks, hold as many as they can, and place them on a table. They should then count the blocks and record the number.

Opportunities can be taken to discuss the fundamentals of 'fair and accurate testing'. For example, the children could think about questions like 'What happens if I drop a block?' and 'How should I grab the blocks?' The idea could even be introduced of having more than one go and recording the highest value.

Once everyone in the class has undertaken this activity, their work can be displayed, showing the hands in order of size along with the number of blocks held by each. This display represents the results of the investigation. Ask the children what they notice: is there a pattern? They may need to be directed to the idea that the bigger hands picked up the most objects. (The pattern can be made more obvious by including older children and adults as test subjects.) Ask the children to try to describe their findings and record their ideas.

DIFFERENTIATION

More able children may be able to produce a graph of their findings. This could be a pictogram with the children's names along one axis and the number of blocks marked with coloured sticky squares of paper. From this graph, they could find out who held the largest number of blocks. They could then investigate whether this person has the biggest hands, by drawing around that person's hand, cutting the shape out and using it to compare to other people's hands.

Less able children may have difficulty dealing with numbers greater than ten. If this is the case, use larger objects, so that fewer can be picked up and therefore fewer have to be counted. Alternatively, use connecting blocks, which can be connected together to make a tower for each person tested. The children can then compare the relative sizes of the towers to determine who picked up the most, rather than having to count the individual blocks.

Now or later

■ Children could carry out another investigation to find out if people's left hands can pick up more than their right hands, or vice versa.
■ Children could write poems about all the things that hands do. These could be written on hand-shaped cut-outs.
■ Children could find out about British sign language, and perhaps learn to 'say' various phrases or even spell out their names.

PLANTS AND LIGHT

INVESTIGATION TYPE:
EXPLORING

RESOURCES AND CLASSROOM ORGANIZATION

Decide if the children will have a container each, or whether they will share one between each group. Prepare the containers as shown in the diagram below before undertaking the activity.

The beginning of this investigation involves lots of discussion that could take place during time in the sitting area of the classroom. The investigation could take place over a number of days, with a different part of the activity being undertaken each day. It is useful to allocate the maintenance duties (for example, watering) to a different group each day.

Each group will need:
■ cress, mustard or grass seeds (a large amount of green manure mustard seed can be purchased cheaply from garden centres)
■ margarine containers with lids
■ cotton wool or kitchen roll
■ water
■ black card or paper
■ sticky tape
■ small spoon
■ 'Plants and light' planning sheets – photocopiable page 18)
■ 'Plants and light' recording sheets – photocopiable page 19).

OBJECTIVES

To give opportunities for children to:
■ understand that collecting evidence is important when trying to answer a question
■ ask questions
■ follow simple instructions
■ make a record of observations
■ relate their findings to what they thought would happen
■ know that plants need light to grow and stay healthy.

VOCABULARY

Conditions, germinate, growth, leaf, light, plants, root, seed, seedling, stem, water.

BACKGROUND KNOWLEDGE

Plants need light to grow and develop into healthy plants – they use the energy from light to make 'food'. Children often develop the misconception that plants get their food from the soil. This investigation will help children alter their ideas about the role soil plays in a plant's life cycle. One of the main functions of soil is to provide a medium in which the roots can become established and hold the plant firm and upright (with the leaves held up towards the light). Soil also holds water, which – along with light and carbon dioxide (a gas from the air) – is required by the plant to make food. Water enters the plant through the roots.

Seeds will germinate in the absence of light, growing thin and yellowish and eventually dying. For seedlings to develop into healthy plants they need light, water and carbon dioxide. Children at KS1 need only to understand that light and water are essential for healthy plant development.

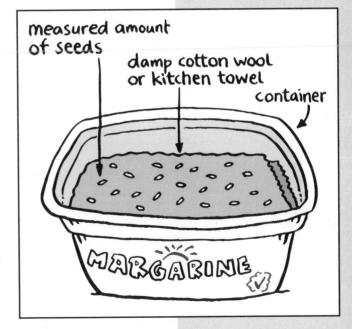

measured amount of seeds

damp cotton wool or kitchen towel

container

MARGARINE ✓

WHAT TO DO

Discuss with the class their ideas about what they need to stay healthy. Get them to think in particular about their diet, where they get their food from, and how it is their food that gives them energy to function. Ask *Where do plants get their food? We never* see *them cooking or in the Supermarket, and they never go to the fish and chip shop!* Many children might suggest that plants get their food from the soil. Some may even say that they have seen plants that catch their food, for example insect-eating plants. Record the children's ideas for later reference. Explain to the class that they are going to undertake an investigation to try to find out 'How plants get food and energy to stay alive and healthy'.

In advance, prepare a number of the containers shown on page 9, as required for the class. Two containers will be used as the 'control' for the investigation: one will be completely covered, letting in no light; the other will be uncovered, letting in

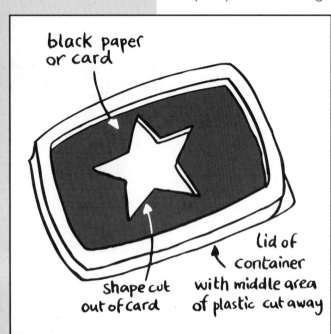

maximum light. Prepare other containers with modified lids as shown below, allowing light to fall on to some areas of the floor of the container but not on to others.

Now, with the children watching, sprinkle an even layer of seeds on to the damp cotton wool or kitchen roll in each container. At this point, elements of 'fair testing' could be discussed. For example, what would happen if all the seeds fell in one place? If the children are ready for this concept, they can record how they made it a 'fair test'.

Ask the children to draw and describe the main features of the setting up of this investigation on the 'Plants and light' planning sheet (photocopiable page 18). They need to label features such as the seeds, the damp cotton wool or kitchen roll and the different-shaped holes to let the light in. They should also consider who will water the plants, and when. Finally, they also need to record an idea of what they think might happen in the containers.

Over the next few days, the children should check the growth of the seedlings and water them carefully with three to four small spoonfuls of water per container every day, and ask the children to record any changes in the development of the seedlings. Ask them questions such as 'Are they all growing the same?', 'How are they growing differently in the different containers?'

After seven or eight days the seedlings should have grown fully. The children should now draw and describe what has happened. Discuss with the class what they think has happened, and remind them about their original ideas. Show them the container that was in full light. As the plants will have grown without soil, and they have not eaten any insects, we can say that plants do not get their food from the soil or by eating insects. So where have the plants got their food? Now show the container in which the seeds grew in darkness. What differences do the children notice? Can they explain these differences? What did the first container have that the second one did not have? The answer is light. Emphasize this point by showing the class the remaining containers. Here they should see that the plants have grown towards the light entering through the cut-out shapes in the lids.

The class should now record their findings by drawing and describing what they have found out, using the 'Plants and light' recording sheet (photocopiable page 19).

DIFFERENTIATION

Less able children may find it easier to consider only the two extremes: of plants grown in full light and plants grown in complete darkness.

More able children could investigate what happens when you change the colour of the light falling on the seedlings. Using coloured filters over the containers, children can observe and compare the effects of different colours of light on plant growth.

NOW OR LATER

■ Children could investigate what happens when they change the amount of water the plants are given. Seeds should be planted in the containers as above, but with equal light falling on each container – only the amount of water given each day should be varied between the containers.

■ Children could make a 'Plant Keep-fit' poster, describing what plants need to stay fit and healthy.

■ Children could plant some sunflower seeds and write a diary of their growth, recording how they have grown and describing the best way to make them grow tall.

SAY IT WITH FLOWERS

INVESTIGATION TYPE:
INVESTIGATING MODELS;
IDENTIFYING AND
CLASSIFYING

RESOURCES AND CLASSROOM ORGANIZATION

This activity can be carried out with children working in small groups or as individuals. A number of flowers will be needed to create a 'garden' for the class to investigate. This investigation can be broken down into two parts. The first part enables children to 'model' flowering plants and label the various parts. The second part involves children surveying their 'virtual garden', identifying plants and recording their numbers.

Each group will need:

■ 'Make your own plants' sheets 1, 2 and 3 – photocopiable pages 20, 21 and 22
■ 'Say it with flowers' recording sheets – photocopiable page 23
■ non-toxic glue
■ scissors
■ colouring pencils or pens
■ card
■ access to a computer with a graphing program (if unavailable or unsuitable, use the 'Say it with flowers' recording sheet – photocopiable page 23)
■ secondary sources, including CD-ROM materials, illustrating flowering plants; for example, seed catalogues, plant identification books
■ potted and cut flowers.

BACKGROUND KNOWLEDGE

Flowers are modified leaves that contain a plant's reproductive organs. Flowers fall mainly into two groups: the small, green, almost unnoticeable flowers of wind-pollinated plants such as grasses, and the spectacular, brightly-coloured flowers of insect-pollinated plants. The stem is the part of the plant that usually grows vertically upwards, towards light. It supports the plant's leaves, buds and flowers. Leaves are the main organs of photosynthesis. They show considerable variation in size, shape and arrangement. Water enters the plant through the roots, and is lost through the leaves. This is called transpiration. Plants do not suck up water.

WHAT TO DO

Discuss with the children their ideas about flowers. Ask them to draw what they think a flower looks like and to label any of the parts with words they know. Keep these initial drawings to use as reference points after the activity, for possible assessment opportunities.

OBJECTIVES

To give opportunities for children to:
■ obtain information from their own work and other simple sources
■ use simple models
■ sort and classify according to simple properties
■ use ICT to present and research information
■ present scientific information in a table and chart
■ recognize and name the leaf, flower, stem and root of a flowering plant.

VOCABULARY

Bulb, flower, fruit, leaf, petal, plants, root, seed, stem.

11

Using the secondary sources and real flowers, allow the children to explore and discover the variety of flowers that exist. Discuss the different parts of plants with them, and introduce words such as leaf, flower, stem and roots. Other words – such as petal, seed, fruit and bulb – might also be within the children's experience and may therefore crop up during discussions.

Explain to the class that they are going to design their own plant. Ask them what 'parts' they will need. Explain that they will need a flower, a stem, some leaves and some roots. This would be a good opportunity to give a simplified explanation of the function of each part. For example, the flower is for making seeds – on many plants, the flowers are brightly coloured and have a pleasant smell to attract insects such as bees, which bring pollen grains from other flowers to help make the seeds. The leaves make food for the plant, using sunlight. The stem supports the flower and the leaves, and the roots hold the whole plant firmly in the soil and let water into the plant.

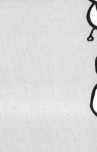

Ask the children to design their own plants, using the 'Make your own plants' sheets 1, 2 and 3 (photocopiable pages 20, 21 and 22). From sheets 1 and 2, a maximum of three plants can be made. The children cut out the parts, and 'mix and match' them to create their own plants. When the children have each created a plant, they can stick them onto copies of sheet 3, and colour in their new creations. This activity can be used to assess each child's learning: has the child used the correct number of parts, can the child name the parts, has the child coloured the leaves in green, and are the roots under the ground level? Ask the children to give each new plant a name and to record the colour of the flower and the number of leaves it has.

Once a number of flowers have been created, the second part of the investigation can take place. Stick the completed plants on to card, and cut them out. Fold the roots to create a base and stick the plants on to a large piece of card, so that they stand up. When this 'virtual garden' been completed the class will be able to carry out the second part of the investigation. The garden can be made more realistic if green paper is used for grass and drops of perfume are used to scent the flowers.

Ask the children to think of some questions about the garden, such as:
■ Which is the most common flower colour in the garden?
■ How many blue flowers are in the garden?
■ How many plants have four leaves?

Once they have decided on a question, ask the children to count the plants, and to record the number(s) they have found. For example, if they have decided to ask 'Which is the most common flower colour?', they should count all the flowers of each colour. This information can either be recorded on the 'Say it with flowers' recording sheet (photocopiable page 23), or keyed into a table in a computer graphing program. From the table, the children can produce a graph, such as a bar graph. Ask them to use the graph to produce a statement that answers their original question. For example

■ 'Red is the most common flower colour in the garden.'
■ 'There are ten blue flowers in the garden.'
■ 'Six plants have only four leaves.'

Finally, refer the children back to their original drawings of flowers. Ask them to draw and label another flower, based on what they have found out from this activity.

DIFFERENTIATION

Less able children may not be able to construct graphs. As an alternative, connecting Maths blocks could be used to represent values; these can be fixed together into towers, so enabling comparisons between values to be made easily.

Looking at pie charts based on the data they have collected could extend more able children.

SAFETY
Children using scissors should be supervised carefully. The glue used should be a suitable non-toxic adhesive.

NOW OR LATER
■ Children could look at real gardens, such as their own. They could use their ideas to design a garden for the school or community.
■ The class could have a competition to see who can grow the tallest sunflower. They could keep a diary of measurements of the length of the stem, or the number of leaves on the plant.
■ The class could extend their virtual garden by including other plants such as trees and shrubs, as well as minibeasts and birds.

PHEW! WHY AM I OUT OF BREATH?

INVESTIGATION TYPE:
FAIR TESTING

RESOURCES AND CLASSROOM ORGANIZATION
The class will need:
■ stopwatches or stopclocks
■ a stethoscope (if possible)
■ 'Phew! Why am I out of breath?' planning and recording sheets – photocopiable page 24
■ PE kit
■ access to a large play area.

OBJECTIVES
To give children opportunities to:
■ be introduced to the idea of a fair test
■ begin to recognize the need for a fair test
■ plan a fair test
■ make simple comparisons.

VOCABULARY
Artery, blood, heart, heartbeat, lungs, muscle, oxygen, pulse, pulse rate, vein.

BACKGROUND KNOWLEDGE
The blood carries important things, like oxygen, to the muscles. The harder the muscles work, the more oxygen they need in order to release energy, so the heart must pump faster. This is why the heart rate increases with exercise. It is the pumping action of the heart that the children can feel or hear. This is called the pulse.

WHAT TO DO
Explain to the class that you have noticed that when people run, they get out of breath. Ask the children if they have noticed this, and whether this is the same for everybody. Ask the children to sit quietly and think about their bodies, about their arms and legs and about their breathing. Ask them to place their hands on their chests, and see if they can feel their heartbeat. Then get them to run on the spot or jump up and down for about one minute. Stop them, and ask what they notice about themselves.

They should be encouraged to notice that they are breathing more quickly. Ask what else happens. Some children may know from experience that other things happen during exercise. For example, their hearts beat faster; they get hot, they sweat, they get tired. It may be necessary to suggest these factors to the children. To draw attention to them, ask the children to feel their chests for their heartbeat (or use the stethoscope, if available), or to listen to one another's chests. The children could also be asked to look at one another to see if they have 'gone red' because they are hot.

Ask the children if they have any ideas why these things happen. Record the children's suggestions and display them so that the class can refer to them later.

Ask 'How could we find out which activity makes our hearts beat the fastest?'

Write a list of activities. These could be suggestions from the class, or else the planning and recording sheet (photocopiable page 24), which suggests some activities, with space to add more ideas. Tell the children that they are going to test each activity. So what will they need to do this?

Get the class to think about:
■ what they will need
■ how they are going to do the activity
■ what they will record.

Ask the children how long they will need to do each activity. Would it matter if somebody did one activity for 10 seconds, whilst somebody else did another activity for 30 seconds? Would this be 'fair'? Discuss with this class why it would not be 'fair', and how they can make sure they carry out a 'fair test'.

Get the class to decide:
■ for how long should they rest between activities (about 1 minute)
■ for how long they will do each activity (about 30 seconds)
■ for how long they will count their heartbeats (about 10 seconds)
(It's best if the teacher controls these times, as they may need to be adjusted in order for the children to obtain reasonable results.) This will generate lots of discussion points about making the test fair.

Ask the children to record their ideas on the planning sheet. Ask them to make a guess about which activity will make their hearts beat the fastest, and (if possible) to suggest a reason for their guess.

Remind the children how to find their pulses by placing one hand firmly on their chests. A sticker could be placed on each child as a reminder of where to place the hand.

During the investigation, encourage children to look at their planning and recording sheets and to discuss their ideas between each other.

Ask the children to record their pulse measurements in the table. Then they should write down their findings using a simple sentence; for example,

'My heart beats fastest when I _____ because _____'.

Once the investigation has been completed, ask each group to contribute to a class bar chart showing the pulse measurements for each activity. Discuss the findings with the class, referring to their ideas and predictions. During these discussions, concepts about exercise, and how vigorous an activity is, can be emphasized to the class. These concepts should be related to health, fitness and diet.

SAFETY
Be aware of and sensitive to any children with lung or heart problems.

DIFFERENTIATION
Less able children might prefer to record direct observations, rather than trying to deal with a fair test.

More able children could plan an investigation using one activity, such as running, over different periods of time (for example, running for 30 seconds, 1 minute, 5 minutes), and comparing the differences. They could see how long it takes for the person's heartbeat to return to normal.

NOW OR LATER
■ The class could make diary of activities that make their hearts beat faster and compare it to a diary of restful activities.
■ The children could take part in a 'health and fitness day'. Here, parents and other guests, such as trainers from a local leisure centre and health visitors, can be invited into school to take part in different activities. The children can put up a display of their work on exercise and heart rate.
■ The children could undertake a survey of parents or older siblings to find out what sports and activities they do in their spare time.
■ The children could visit a local leisure centre and experience a wide range of activities.

SNACK ATTACK!

INVESTIGATION TYPE:
PATTERN SEEKING

RESOURCES AND CLASSROOM ORGANIZATION
This investigation is ideally suited to children working in small groups. Birds that appear in the playground are chosen as subjects for this investigation. If this is impractical, use snails or slugs, kept in a plastic tank in the classroom. Do not use crisps as a food source for snails or slugs; the salt will kill them. Instead, try small pieces of fruit and vegetables as a food source. If snails or slugs are used, consideration must be given to the welfare of the animals in the classroom, and children must wash their hands thoroughly after handling the animals.
Each group will need:
■ a bird table or similar area on which to place food samples
■ 'Snack attack!' planning sheets – photocopiable page 25
■ a variety of flavoured crisps
■ weighing scales (capable of measuring 10g; digital scales are ideal)
■ lids from margarine tubs.

OBJECTIVES
To give children opportunities to:
■ ask questions about ideas in science
■ turn ideas suggested into a form that can be investigated
■ make observations and measurements
■ use their results to say what they found out
■ find out about different kinds of animals in the local environment.

VOCABULARY
Bird, environment, food, plan.

BACKGROUND KNOWLEDGE
Crisps are obviously not a natural food source for birds, but the fact that birds eat them – and that in many school playgrounds they wait for playtimes to finish to pick up the scraps – shows how animals have learned to adapt to co-exist with humans. This behaviour also illustrates how easily humans influence the environment and how we must therefore take great care and consider carefully the effects of our actions.

WHAT TO DO
Ask the children if they have ever noticed birds picking up the crumbs left after playtime. It would be useful if the class could observe this. (Strategically place some crisps or breadcrumbs in the playground before asking the children to watch, to ensure that some birds will appear!)
Back in the classroom, ask the class to plan a science investigation to find out which crisps the birds on the playground like the best. This could be done as a whole-class brainstorm activity, or as a small group activity.

The children need to consider:
■ what flavour crisps to use
■ how many of each flavour to use
■ how to measure how much has been eaten
■ how long they will observe for.

Ask the children to record their ideas by drawing or writing on the 'Snack attack!' planning sheet (photocopiable page 25).

As this investigation encourages children to plan, most of the teacher input will occur during this stage. Young children can offer a huge range of different ideas, but allowing every child to carry out his or her own investigation separately could be problematic. In order to promote an environment in which children can freely express their ideas, and to provide evidence for assessment purposes, the teacher could allow everyone the opportunity to describe their plans to the rest of the class. Discuss the ideas and suggestions with the class, and draw out important points to construct a plan to which all the children feel as though they have contributed. For this investigation, a plan could follow these lines.

1 Identify an area that birds visit – the playground after playtimes is ideal.
2 Weigh out a fixed amount of each of the different flavoured crisps (10g for example, or use one packet) and place each flavour on a separate margarine tub lid.
3 Place the lids in the area to be observed and set a time limit of about 15 minutes, during which time the class could observe from a window. (If there are a lot of birds, a shorter time will be needed; if there are few birds, allow a longer observation period.)
4 Afterwards, bring the samples back to the classroom and carefully weigh them using digital scales. (If digital scales are not available, then a visual judgement could be used).
5 Discuss the result with the children. Is there any pattern that suggests the birds might like one flavour more than another? Of course, there is no guarantee that the birds will show any preference, or even eat any at all. Whatever pattern emerges, devise with the children a simple sentence that describes it, such as

'The birds we saw ate more _____ flavour crisps than any other, so they might like this flavour best'.

DIFFERENTIATION

Less able children may not be able to plan effectively, so they could be asked to record simple observations instead, with strategic questions asked at relevant points, for example, 'Why do you think we put each flavour food in separate containers and not all in one bowl?'

More able children could devise their own questions about birds visiting the school grounds. They could think about recording the different types of birds that visit, or testing different types of food such as bread or nuts.

SAFETY

Make sure children wash their hands thoroughly after handling any food that has been in contact with animals.

NOW OR LATER

■ Children could carry out a survey of the favourite snacks eaten at playtimes in the school.
■ The class could link with other schools, through e-mail or fax, and ask the children there to carry out the same investigation to see what flavour crisps the birds like in their area.
■ Children could plan an investigation to find out the favourite foods of other animals, such as snails, slugs, rabbits, hamsters or guinea pigs.

Handy hands planning and recording sheet

Place a hand in the box and draw around it.

How many will this hand be able to hold?

How many did this hand hold?

In my class, _____ picked up the most.

Plants and light 1: planning sheet

These are the things I will use in my investigation:

Draw your investigation:

Describe what you think might happen. You can draw a picture.

Plants and light 2: recording sheet

This what happened in my investigation.

I think this happened because:

Name

Date

Say it with flowers:
Make your own plants 1

Flowers

Stems

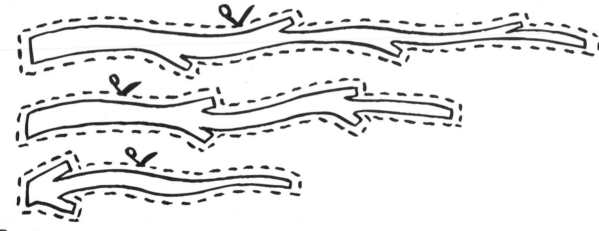

Roots

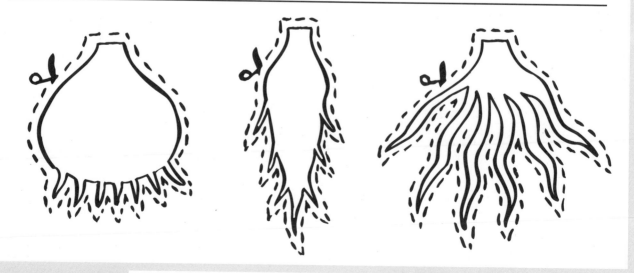

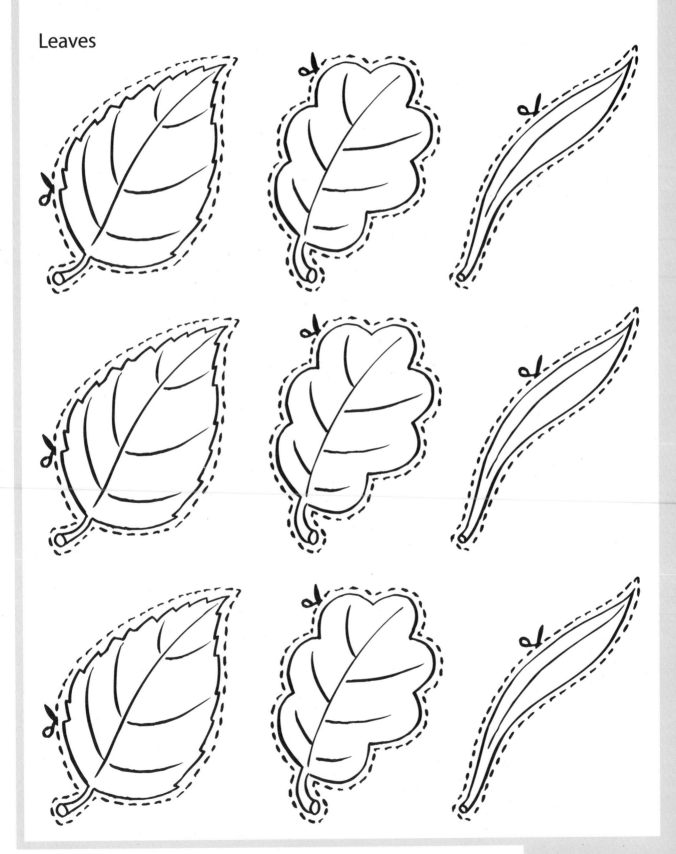
Say it with flowers:
Make your own plants 2

Leaves

Say it with flowers:
Make your own plants 3

Put your plant in the garden.

This plant is called _____.

The colour of its flower is _____.

It has _____ leaves.

Ready to go! IDEAS FOR SCIENCE INVESTIGATIONS

Say it with flowers: recording sheet

Put the data you have collected into the table. Use the information to draw a graph.

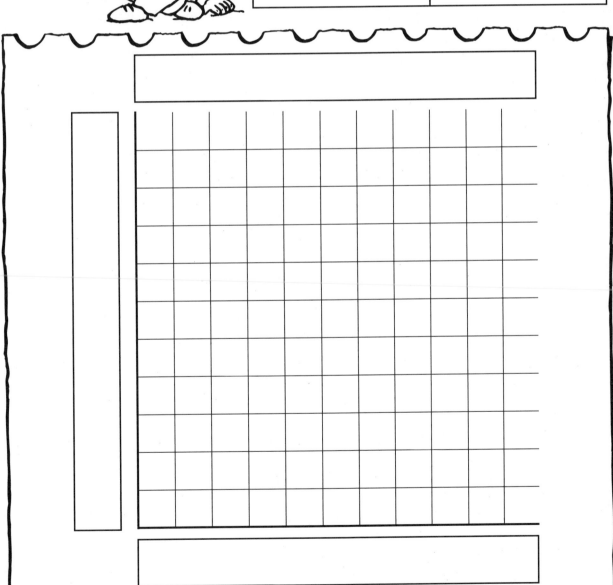

Ready to go! IDEAS FOR SCIENCE INVESTIGATIONS

Name _____   Date _____

Phew! Why am I out of breath?
Planning and recording sheet

We are going to do each activity for _____.

We are going to rest for _____.

We are going to measure _____.

We will need these things:

I think _____

will make my heart beat the slowest because:

I think _____

will make my heart beat the fastest because:

Activity	My heartbeat
Sitting down	
Running	
Walking	
Jumping	
Lying down	
Standing still	
Rolling	
Reading	
Hopping	

This is what I looked like after running:

My heart beats fastest when I

_____

because:

Name   Date

Snack attack! planning sheet

We are trying to find out

I think the birds will like _____
the best.

These are the things I will need:

This is what I will do:

This section relates to the Programme of Study: Materials and their properties (Sc3). Here children begin to develop skills they need to ask questions, observe and explore ideas about a wide range of materials. Through the investigations described in this section, children can explore the properties of a variety of everyday materials, and learn to describe their ideas by developing a scientific vocabulary using drawings, charts and tables. The activities encourage a 'hands on' approach, providing children with a wider sensory experience to encourage their scientific thinking. They are also asked to consider the safety implications of their investigative work, to themselves and to others.

SKIPPING TEST

INVESTIGATION TYPE:
EXPLORING

OBJECTIVES
To give children opportunities to:
■ use simple scientific language to communicate ideas
■ make recordings of observations and comparisons
■ develop ideas about 'fair testing'
■ find out how objects can be changed by processes
■ find out about the uses of a variety of materials.

VOCABULARY
Cloth, clothes, compare, fabric, fair test, fibres, materials, natural, strength, synthetic.

RESOURCES AND CLASSROOM ORGANIZATION
Collect together various clothing fabrics. (School jumble sales make an ideal source of fabrics to use.) Divide the class into groups.
Each group will need:
■ samples of clothing fabrics (preferably two of each fabric)
■ a skipping rope
■ access to an open space with a rough floor surface, such as the playground
■ 'Skipping test' planning and recording sheets – photocopiable page 38
■ masking tape
■ hand lenses.

BACKGROUND KNOWLEDGE
Most clothes are made from fabrics woven from different types of fibres. These fibres may be made from natural materials such as wool, cotton or silk, or from synthetic materials such as nylon, polyester or viscose. All these materials are made into long thin fibres by a manufacturing process. These fibres are then woven together to make the fabrics used to make clothes.

WHAT TO DO
Discuss with the class their ideas about the function of clothes. They might suggest that we wear clothes to keep warm, or that some clothes are waterproof, but they may not have considered that clothes need to be strong. Discuss with the class possible reasons for this – clothes get pulled and stretched, they get rubbed as we move and they get really bashed about in the washing machine and tumble dryer.

Explain to the class that they are going to test some fabrics to find out what happens when they are rubbed a lot. You could ask the children for their ideas about how they could do this. Explain to them that you have thought of a way of making sure the fabric gets rubbed the same amount each time: one member of each group is going to skip with the material attached to his or her shoe. Explain that they must test each material with the same number of skips. At this point opportunities can be taken to discuss with the children how this would make the test fair.

Each group needs to have somebody to do the skipping. Using the masking tape, attach the sample of fabric to the sole of the child's shoe. Before they do the test, ask the children to

describe what they think might happen. They should record their ideas on the 'Skipping test' planning and recording sheet (photocopiable page 38). It would be useful to have two samples of the fabric to be tested, so that 'before and after' comparisons can be made later.

Ask the children to carry out the test on a hard, rough surface such as the playground. Remind the children of the decisions they made about how they would do this; for example, that they must use the same number of skips each time. Once all the fabrics have been tested, the children can examine the samples. Encourage them to look really closely for the changes that have taken place. Hand lenses or magnifying glasses could be used to help draw the children's attention to the structure of the fabric.

Ask the class to record their observations using drawings and descriptive writing on the 'Skipping test' planning and recording sheet. They could describe the fabrics before and after the test. Using the findings of the class as a whole, the children can try to place the range of fabrics they have investigated into order, from 'toughest' to 'weakest'. This can be done in small groups, where the children can discuss and explore their results, and try to think of possible explanations. Children should identify that the combination of what a fabric is made from and how it is woven together gives the cloth its strength properties. Using this knowledge, the children could be asked what materials they would use to make clothes for people doing particular jobs; for example, for a gardener, mechanic, teacher, ballet dancer or footballer.

DIFFERENTIATION

Some children may not have the co-ordination skills required to skip. If required, the testing process can be replaced by any activity that involves the fabrics being rubbed vigorously. This could include jumping or running, or using sandpaper to make the activity purely classroom-based.

SAFETY

The skipping activity should take place outside, and the children should be aware of the safety issue raised by swinging the skipping rope when other people are around.

NOW OR LATER

■ Children can think of other properties of fabrics to investigate, such as how waterproof they are or which would be the best at keeping us warm or cool. Children could offer their own ideas about how they could go about investigating these properties. There is no need to actually carry out the investigations, but discuss with the children their reasons for the choices they have made. For example, discuss the equipment they would use, how they would make it a 'fair test', how they would make the test safe, and what sort of results they might get.

■ The class could investigate the processes involved in making fabrics. They could learn about the origins of natural materials such as wool from sheep, silk from the cocoons of the silk moth and cotton from cotton plants. They could make a simple contrast with the manufacturing process of nylon, for example.

■ Children could try their hand at spinning or knitting and make observations of how the properties of the material change.

Oh dear! mop it up!

INVESTIGATION TYPE:
FAIR TESTING

OBJECTIVES

To give children opportunities to:
■ use their experiences to develop their own scientific ideas
■ use drawings to present scientific information
■ suggest what might happen in an investigation
■ make simple comparisons
■ recognize that a comparison may not always be fair.

VOCABULARY

Absorb, material, mop, paper, soak up, soaked, towel.

RESOURCES AND CLASSROOM ORGANIZATION

For this investigation the children will need to work in small groups, but record their ideas individually.

Each group will need:

■ a variety of materials that could be used to 'mop up'; for example, paper towels, kitchen towel, all-purpose kitchen cloths, sponge, silver foil, cling film, polythene
■ clear plastic beakers
■ strips of coloured paper
■ countdown timer or stopclock
■ 'Mop it up!' planning and recording sheets – photocopiable page 39.

BACKGROUND KNOWLEDGE

Capillary action occurs because water is 'sticky'. The water molecules stick to each other and to other materials, such as glass or cloth. Dip a paper towel into a glass of water and the water will 'climb' onto the paper. It will keep going up the towel until the pull of gravity is too much for it to overcome.

Capillary action is important for moving water. It is defined as the movement of water within the spaces of a porous material due to the forces of adhesion, cohesion, and surface tension.

Materials that are made up of fibres such as cloth or paper have lots of spaces and surfaces for water to stick to and move through. The more fibrous a material is the more water it can absorb. Paper can be treated to repel water; for example, greaseproof paper.

WHAT TO DO

Spill some water on a desk and ask the children *What should I do?* They will probably suggest that you should mop it up, perhaps using a paper towel. Ask the children to watch very carefully what happens when you mop up the mess. What happens to the paper towel and the water? Squeeze the towel – what happens? Ask for their ideas about this.

Could you use any other materials to do the same job? How could they find out which material would make a good 'mopper'? They could test different materials to see how much water each one soaked up from a beaker.

Ask the children, working in groups, how they could make this a 'fair test'. They will need to keep the following factors the same:

■ the size of each piece of material

■ the amount of water in each beaker (do not fill the beakers, as the water will overflow; about half full should be sufficient)
■ the length of time for which each piece of material is left in the water.
For each different material used, the children should measure the amount of water left in the beaker after the agreed time (the smallest amount left indicates the most absorbent material).

Once these criteria have been discussed and decided upon, write them on a large piece of paper and display it so the group will be reminded what to do. Before carrying out the investigation, allow the group to explore and examine the materials. Discuss with the group the properties of the materials and ask them to predict which material they think will absorb the most water, giving a reason for their choice. Ask them to record their ideas on the 'Mop it up!' planning and recording sheet (photocopiable page 39).

Next, the children should carry out the investigation by placing each sample of material in a beaker of water. After the agreed time (about 2 minutes), they should carefully remove the material, and allow the surplus water to run off back into the beaker. They should make a note of, and label the beaker with, the name of the material tested, and put the beaker to one side. This should be repeated with all the selected materials.

Once the testing has been completed the measuring can begin. Make sure the children understand that the beaker with the smallest amount of water left in it shows the material that absorbed the most. The results can be recorded in a number of ways. Through observation the beakers could be placed in order, from 'most absorbed' to 'least absorbed'. This order could then be recorded as a list, with the most effective 'mopper' at the top and the least effective at the bottom (see photocopiable page 39). Strips of coloured paper the same height as the depth of the water in each beaker can be used to create a more graphical representation. Longer strips should be placed next to each beaker, the water level marked and the strip cut to the right length, so indicating the amount of water left. These strips can be stuck down to make a simple bar graph.

Ask the group to think about and discuss their results. Do they differ from their predictions, and if so, how? Can they think of some ideas about the how the properties of a material (such as hardness, stiffness, appearance) might affect its ability to absorb water.

DIFFERENTIATION

More able children could investigate different types or thicknesses of kitchen roll, for example two/three/four-ply. They could use more accurate measuring devices – for example, a measuring cylinder – to determine which sample absorbs the most water.

Less able children would benefit from having to test fewer materials, which have more obvious properties related to absorption; for example, a thick sponge cloth, a paper towel and cling film. These would give results of 'good', 'medium' and 'poor' absorbency, helping children to identify the link between the property of the material and its ability to absorb water.

SAFETY

Remind the children that although this activity might be fun, they must still remember that they have a responsibility to carry out the investigation carefully and sensibly.

NOW OR LATER

■ Children could repeat the above investigation, using a different liquid such as paint or milk instead of water. Will the results be different?
■ Children could find out how changing the size of the material sample used will affect how much it absorbs.
■ Children could find out how many cups of water a disposable nappy will absorb, and compare different types. Ask the children to guess how much a nappy will hold.
■ Children could test different brands of kitchen towel to see if they are as good as the advertisements claim.

STICKY STUFF

INVESTIGATION TYPE:
PATTERN SEEKING

OBJECTIVES

To give children opportunities to:
■ ask questions about their ideas in science
■ explore using appropriate senses
■ make observations and measurements
■ make simple comparisons
■ try to explain what they have found out.

VOCABULARY

Dough, flour, sticky, stretch, water.

RESOURCES AND CLASSROOM ORGANIZATION

This can be a messy activity, so it must take place in a suitable area, with the children wearing aprons. It is also recommended that the teacher experiments in advance to determine suitable amounts of flour and water to create the different consistencies of dough. When making the dough, add the water to the flour, rather than vice versa. During this investigation, the children can work in small groups, with each group working on its own sequence of bowls (although the teacher may prefer to carry out a teacher demonstration instead!).

Each group will need:
■ plain flour
■ water
■ plastic mixing bowls
■ weighing scales
■ tablespoons or measuring scoops
■ 'Sticky stuff' recording sheets – photocopiable page 40
■ plastic shape cutters.

BACKGROUND KNOWLEDGE

When flour and water are mixed they form a simple dough. The water is absorbed by the particles of flour making them swell, so the dough becomes stretchy and sticky. Varying the proportion of water in the mixture will alter the properties of the dough and the ways it behaves.

WHAT TO DO

Mix two examples of dough, one with lots of water so that it is stretchy and sticky, and the other with very little water, which makes it dry and easily broken. Show the class the ingredients that you used to make the doughs. Allow the children to explore the doughs, and ask them to describe the differences between the two types. Ask the class for their suggestions of why they behave differently.

Explain that they are going to investigate what happens when different amounts of water are used to make the dough. Ask the children to think about what will happen. Will more water make the dough more stretchy or less stretchy?

Prepare a number of bowls with a fixed amount of flour in each (for example, 200g). With the children, decide how much water to add to the first bowl. Gradually increase the amount added to each successive bowl. (The teacher will need to test and identify suitable values in advance.) In each bowl, mix the flour and water and allow the children to explore and examine the new mixture.

Ask the children to compare the new mixture with the previous one. Is it more or less stretchy? Is it more or less sticky? What will the next mixture in the sequence be like? As more water is added to each subsequent mixture, they should become stickier. If children have not already observed it, highlight this pattern to them through questioning. Ask them to make observational drawings and encourage them to think of as many words as they can to describe the different mixtures. They can record their ideas on the 'Sticky stuff' recording sheet (photocopiable page 40).

DIFFERENTIATION

More able children could repeat the investigation using different types of flour or using warm water.

Less able children would benefit from having fewer mixtures to compare, with the pattern made more obvious; for example, using tiny, moderate and large amounts of water.

SAFETY

Remind the children that although they are using food ingredients for their science work, they should never put anything in their mouth and should never eat when undertaking science work. Ensure that the bowls used are not breakable.

NOW OR LATER

■ The teacher could make a fun mixture as a demonstration for the class, which they could call 'Stretchy stuff'. Ask the children to describe the different ingredients. What do they think the mixture will turn out like?

1 Measure out one level teaspoon of talcum powder and place it in a plastic cup.

2 Add 10cm^3 of moisturising lotion (this must be oil free, baby lotion is ideal), 10cm^3 of PVA glue and 10cm^3 of water. Stir well to mix the ingredients.

3 Add 5cm^3 of 5% Borax solution and stir. (Borax is available from pharmacies: to make a 5% solution mix 5ml of Borax into 100ml of water. You may need to vary the concentration to obtain the best results.)

4 Remove the Stretchy stuff from the cup. Once the mixture is made, the class can stretch, bend and even bounce it!

■ Children could make salt dough models.

■ Children could make bread or cakes and see how applying heat can further change the consistency of the mixtures.

BUBBLES!

RESOURCES AND CLASSROOM ORGANIZATION

This can be a messy activity so it must take place in a suitable area, with the children wearing aprons. Create a 'Bubble Exploration Centre' that contains a wide variety of objects for the children to use to explore bubbles. During this investigation the children can work in small groups.

Each group will need:

■ objects to make bubble blowers; for example, plastic straws, colanders, sieves, large paper clips, string, plastic film canisters with holes in the base (these make very good bubble blowers), anything you can blow through (try old plastic musical instruments).

■ bottles of bubble solution (bought from toy shops)

■ wire coat hangers

■ corks

■ plastic insulating tape

■ a number of plastic bowls

■ two to three cups of washing up liquid

■ 4.5 litres of water

■ two to three tablespoons of glycerine (available from pharmacies)

■ a camera and film (to record the children working)

■ safety goggles

■ aprons

■ 'Bubbles!' recording sheets – photocopiable page 41.

BACKGROUND KNOWLEDGE

The physical interaction of the molecules of the detergent and the molecules of water form the skin of a bubble, this skin is extremely stretchy. If you blow a bubble

INVESTIGATION TYPE:
EXPLORING

OBJECTIVES

To give children opportunities to:

■ ask questions about their ideas in science

■ explore using appropriate senses

■ make simple comparisons

■ try and explain what they found out

VOCABULARY

Bubble, colours, rainbow, soap, water.

and close the opening, the tension in the bubble skin tries to shrink the bubble into a shape with the smallest possible surface area for the volume of air it contains. That shape happens to be a sphere. The way the surface of the bubble reflects light means that it is divided into the colours of the spectrum or rainbow. The surface of the bubble is liquid so the colours move and swirl. Bubbles are formed when a gas is released into a liquid.

WHAT TO DO

Beforehand, mix a large amount of bubble solution and bend the wire coat hangers into different shapes. Place a cork on the pointed end of each, and cover with plastic insulating tape. Bundle some straws together and secure with tape to make multi-bubble blowers. Tie lots of knotted loops in a piece of string.

At the beginning of the lesson, begin with the whole class. Ask the children to watch very carefully as you blow bubbles over them. Promise them that after they have watched carefully they can try to burst them, but first they must watch carefully. Ask them to think about:

■ what shapes the bubbles make
■ what colours they can see
■ what happens when the bubbles burst.

Ask the class to think of words to describe what they observe. Write these down and display them in the 'Bubble Exploration Centre'.

Divide the class into groups when they are ready to undertake the investigation. As well as 'free-play exploration', set the children a number of tasks to try to achieve. Ask them to:

■ make a bubble using only their hands
■ make the biggest bubble they can
■ catch a bubble without it bursting
■ find out how many bubbles they can make with one blow.

Whilst children are exploring, ask lots of questions about the nature of the bubbles they create. Use a camera to take photographs of the children in action.

After the investigation ask the children to record their ideas on the 'Bubbles!' recording sheet (photocopiable page 41).

SAFETY

Soap solution can irritate the eyes, so it is advisable that children wear safety goggles during this activity. Teachers should be aware of any children who are sensitive to soap as an irritant to the skin; such children could wear rubber gloves. Children should be aware that spillages might make the floor slippery.

NOW OR LATER

■ Children could mix a soap solution with paint and make bubble pictures.
■ Put some pondweed (available from pet shops) in a clear container, and place it in a well-lit area. The children can watch as the plants produce oxygen bubbles. Then look at other bubbles by mixing baking powder (Bicarbonate of Soda) and vinegar, or by observing the bubbles in fizzy drinks.
■ Children could try to make huge bubbles using a small paddling pool containing bubble solution and a PE hoop. Or they could use a tennis racket to create millions of tiny bubbles.
■ Children could make a collection of materials that have bubbles in them; for example, sponge, bread, bubble wrap.

A FISH OUT OF WATER!

RESOURCES AND CLASSROOM ORGANIZATION

The investigation will take a number of days to get any results. It is best organized either as a whole-class activity, or as a group activity to take place over a number of weeks. Otherwise the classroom will be full of water-filled containers, and spillage will be inevitable.

Each group will need:
■ empty margarine containers (must all be the same size)
■ silver foil
■ access to a fridge
■ water
■ measuring cylinder
■ 'A fish out of water!' recording sheets – photocopiable page 42
■ plastic pop bottles.

BACKGROUND KNOWLEDGE

Evaporation is the process by which a liquid changes state into a gas at a temperature below the liquid's boiling point. Evaporation takes place at the surface of the liquid, so the larger the surface area, the greater the opportunity for evaporation to take place. Moving molecules at the surface of the liquid escape into the air. Any activity that increases this movement, such as an increase in temperature or air movements above the liquid's surface, will increase the rate at which the liquid evaporates.

Evaporation is a physical change and is reversible. The reverse process, from gas to liquid, is called condensation. Both evaporation and condensation play important roles in the water cycle.

WHAT TO DO

Discuss with the class where they think the best place to put a fish bowl would be. For example, would it be best to put it on a shelf, on a radiator, on a window ledge, or in a fridge? What do they think would happen to the water in the bowl in each of the different places?

Set up a bowl in each location, with the same amount of water in each. Make fish shapes out of silver foil and place one in each bowl. (This is only for effect, but could be used later to see if bowls with more fish dry up more quickly.) Mark the water level and place each bowl in the chosen position. Set a time limit of one to two days. After this time, ask the children to look at each bowl. What has happened to the water? The water levels should have gone down – in the bowl on the radiator, the water may well have dried up completely. In this case, what would have happened to the fish?

The children should look at two points from this investigation. The first is that the water has not disappeared, but has changed and is now in the air – it will eventually turn into clouds and fall back to the ground as rain. Children might find this concept difficult to understand or even believe, but the process of condensation can be easily illustrated as follows. Half fill some plastic pop bottles with water, seal them and place them in a fridge until cold; then place the bottles on a warm radiator and, after 10–15 minutes the children should see droplets of water condensing from the classroom air and forming on the sides of the bottles.

OBJECTIVES
To give children opportunities to:
■ ask questions about their ideas in science
■ make simple comparisons
■ make simple observations
■ use their results to say what they have found out
■ describe the way some everyday materials change when they are heated or cooled.

VOCABULARY
Air, cold, cool, dry, evaporation, liquid, water, warm.

Encourage the children to describe what happened in terms such as 'The water dried up and went into the air'. Explain to the class that in science we use a special word to describe this process: the word is 'evaporation'.

The second point is to try to identify a simple pattern in the results. Highlight to the children that the water levels in the bowls in the warm areas went down more quickly than those in the cold areas. Ask them to produce sentences to describe this. They may use statements such as 'When it is warm the water dries up quicker', 'The warm radiator makes water dry up more quickly', or 'When it is cold, water doesn't dry up very quickly'. By describing their observations in this way, the children are describing a pattern. Children can record their ideas on the 'A fish out of water!' recording sheet (photocopiable page 42). They can apply what they have seen to other situations such as puddles in the playground or washing on a clothes line.

The children can use the information from the investigation to decide the best place to position the fish bowl. If they place it somewhere too warm, the water will dry up and the fish will die. On the other hand, if the bowl is placed in the fridge, the fish will be too cold.

DIFFERENTIATION

More able children could measure and record how much water is lost from each bowl over time. They could do this by marking the water level at set times.

Less able children may be distracted by the use of the goldfish; therefore, undertake the investigation without this additional 'context' detail.

SAFETY

Remind children of the importance of working sensibly, carefully and responsibly, especially as they are working with water: spilling the water would not only cause a mess, and make the floor dangerously slippery, but it could also mean that the results of the investigation are spoiled.

NOW OR LATER

■ Children could design their own fish tanks, and include ideas to help with the care of the fish, as well as ways of stopping the water from evaporating (for example, they could use a lid).

■ Get a real fish tank with goldfish for the classroom.

■ Children could investigate how puddles on the playground dry up. After it has rained, draw around a puddle with chalk. Continue this process at set time intervals until the puddle has dried up completely. Children could predict whether larger or smaller puddles would dry up first, and then investigate to find out.

ANNIE'S TIGHTS

INVESTIGATION TYPE:
FAIR TESTING

OBJECTIVES

To give children opportunities to:

■ ask questions about their ideas in science

■ present scientific information in a table

■ sort and classify scientific information

■ make an appropriate record of observations

■ recognize that a test or comparison may not always be fair.

RESOURCES AND CLASSROOM ORGANIZATION

For this investigation, the children can work in small groups.
Each group will need:

■ three pairs of children's tights, of various thicknesses

■ 1kg weight (a bag of sugar is ideal)

■ measuring tape

■ strips of paper (used for recording measurements)

■ Maths blocks (used for recording measurements)

■ 'Annie's tights' recording sheets – photocopiable page 43.

BACKGROUND KNOWLEDGE

When a weight is hung from a pair of tights, gravity pulls the weight down. As it does so, it applies a force to the tights and makes them stretch. The material of which the tights are made has elastic properties, and therefore applies an opposing force, stopping the weight from falling. This is a bit like a tug-of-war between the 'down' pull of gravity and the 'up' pull of the tights. Once the weight is removed, the material returns to its normal size. As tights are made in different thicknesses, they will take different amounts of force to stretch them. The thicker they are, the more they oppose the force pulling down, so the less they will stretch.

WHAT TO DO

Put the investigation into context by telling the children a short story about Annie.

"Annie is a little girl who has only just learned to dress herself. She feels very grown up. She can even tie her shoelaces all on her own. Isn't she clever? Every morning Annie's Mum puts out the clothes she is going to wear that day – her vest, pants, skirt, jumper and Annie's favourite piece of clothing, her tights.

Annie likes her tights because they look ever so small in the drawer, but when she puts them on she can push with her toes and pull them right up to her waist and – as if by magic – they fit perfectly.

One day, Annie's mum forgot to put her tights out. As it was rather chilly outside, Annie decided that she would pick a pair of tights herself. She opened the drawer of her wardrobe and looked inside. There were lots of different tights. They all looked the same size, so Annie pulled out a pair. But when she put them on she could only pull them up to her knees – they wouldn't stretch any further. Annie quickly took them off and tried another pair, but this time when she tried them they stretched right up to her nose. 'HELP!' cried Annie. In came Annie's mum and laughed 'Oh Annie, you have got the wrong size there!. Here are your tights.'

'But they all look the same to me!' exclaimed Annie.

'I know, but different tights stretch differently. Now, come on, hurry up or we will be late for school'.

On the way to school Annie thought about why the tights all stretched differently. She decided that when she got to school she would ask her teacher and friends to help her find out more. They could do a science investigation.

Can you help Annie plan an investigation to find out why the tights all stretched differently?"

With a group of children, introduce and describe the equipment they will need for the investigation. Look at the different pairs of tights. What are the differences? What are the similarities? Demonstrate to the group that you can alter the stretch by applying a larger or smaller force.

So, do they think Annie just pulled harder with some tights than with others? Is that why they stretched differently, or could there be something different about the tights themselves? Look at the tights closely and ask the children about the thickness, the materials and even the colour. Could these have any effect on what happened? Explain that the test must be fair: each pair of tights must be stretched with the same kind of force. Otherwise, as they have already seen, the size of the force affects how much things stretch. By using the downward pull created by a 1kg weight (bag of sugar), the force will be kept the same for each pair of tights.

Before undertaking the investigation, ask the children which pair they think will stretch the most. Why do they think this?

Label each pair of tights (for example, Pair 1, Pair 2, Pair 3) and then children can begin the testing. They should hold the tights up to see how big they are, then put the bag of sugar down one leg and measure the difference in length between the legs. They can use a strip of paper or Maths blocks to record this length.

35

Once all three pairs of tights have been tested, children should compare the measurements. Which pair has stretched the most? Are the results different to their predictions? Ask the children to record their ideas and thoughts about possible reasons for the results. This can be done using the 'Annie's tights' recording sheet (photocopiable page 43). The results can be displayed as large bar graphs, using the strips of paper or drawing around the towers of block to create the bars.

After the investigation has finished, discuss with the children how they might be able to improve the investigation. Such improvements could involve using different types of tights, repeating measurements, measuring the differences using standard units, or measuring the pull using forcemeters.

DIFFERENTIATION

More able children could draw their own simple bar graphs to represent the results, or test more pairs of tights.

Less able children could test just one pair of tights by seeing how far they will stretch, so developing the concept of the relationship between the size of a force and the stretch it causes.

SAFETY

Remind the children about the risks involved in stretching things and suddenly letting them go. They should also be urged to take great care with the kilogram weight, to avoid dropping it on toes or fingers.

NOW OR LATER

■ Children could make a collection of stretchy and non-stretchy materials. Which one stretches the most?
■ Children could draw patterns and pictures on balloons, to see what happens to the pictures when the balloons are inflated.
■ Children could act out or paint pictures telling Annie's story, and how the class explained the problem.

MR FREEZE

(This activity has been adapted from 'The Iceman Cometh' by Anne Goldsworthy, in *The Times Educational Supplement – Primary Magazine*, January 1998.)

INVESTIGATION TYPE:
PATTERN SEEKING

OBJECTIVES
To give children opportunities to:
■ ask questions about their ideas in science
■ use their experiences and the information they obtain from their investigations to develop their own scientific ideas
■ describe their work clearly using appropriate vocabulary
■ explore using appropriate senses
■ make simple comparisons
■ use their results to say what they have found out.

VOCABULARY
Cold, freeze, ice, insulate, melt, warm, water.

RESOURCES AND CLASSROOM ORGANIZATION
This investigation needs to be prepared beforehand. Fill the rubber gloves with tap water and place in a freezer overnight. When ready to use, run the gloves under warm water, carefully cut away the gloves and you will have two ice 'hands'.
Each group will need:
■ a pair of rubber gloves
■ plastic trays
■ bubble wrap
■ stopclock or stopwatch
■ 'Mr Freeze' recording sheet – photocopiable page 44
■ 'Mr Freeze goes on holiday' playscript - photocopiable pages 45 and 46.

BACKGROUND KNOWLEDGE
When ice melts, it absorbs heat from the surroundings. Heat will always be conducted from a warm object to a cold one. When the ice is wrapped in a material, this affects how the heat is absorbed. Materials such as bubble wrap act as insulators, slowing down this transfer of heat energy. As a result, ice wrapped in bubble wrap will melt more slowly than ice left in warm air without insulation. We often tell children to put their coats on to keep warm – this can give children the erroneous

impression that the coat material has a warming effect, so when ice is wrapped in a material they think it should melt more quickly. In fact, the opposite happens, because the material acts as a barrier slowing down the transfer of heat.

WHAT TO DO

Show the class the two ice 'hands' – they are a snowman's spare hands. Ask the children what they think would happen if they left them out in the classroom. They should suggest that the hands would melt. Explain that the snowman would like to take these spare hands on holiday. Can they think of any way of stopping the ice from melting so quickly? Suggest that they could wrap one in bubble wrap. Do they think this will help?

Wrap one hand in a few layers of bubble wrap (or any material that is a good thermal insulator) and leave the other uncovered. Ask the children to predict which one they think will melt the quickest. They can record their predictions on the 'Mr Freeze' recording sheet (photocopiable page 44).

The hands should be left in a warm room. Use a stopclock to time how quickly the melting takes place, but simple observations will suffice as a record of the results. If possible, take photographs or use a video camera to record the changes.

After a period of time the children should notice the hands melting. Remove the bubble wrap and compare both hands. Ask the children to describe what has happened. They can make observational drawings and record their ideas on the 'Mr Freeze' recording sheet (photocopiable page 44).

DIFFERENTIATION

More able children could use lengths of string to measure around the ice hands. This would provide a measurable record of how the size changes. The lengths of string could be stuck on to card to show a record of the changes, or measured using non-standard or standard units and then used to plot a bar graph.

SAFETY

Children should avoid touching very cold objects – that is, objects directly from a freezer – as this offers a risk to them and can harm their skin. It is advisable to wear gloves when handling very cold objects.

NOW OR LATER

Use the play 'Mr Freeze goes on holiday' (photocopiable pages 45 and 46), to reinforce the concepts covered in this activity.

Skipping test: planning and recording sheet

Draw and write about the fabrics you are investigating.

Fabric:	Fabric:
Fabric:	**Fabric:**
Fabric:	**Fabric:**

Mop it up! planning and recording sheet

How I made this test fair:

Draw your investigation.

The materials I tested:

▼ best 'mopper' ▼
▲ worst 'mopper' ▲

The best 'mopper' was _____. I think this is because

Name   Date

Sticky stuff: recording sheet

Draw pictures of the dough you have made.

This mixture is

This mixture is

When I make a dough using more water, the dough is

_____.

I think this happens because

Name

Date

Bubbles! recording sheet

Draw some of the bubbles you made.

Describe how you made bubbles.

Name

Date

A fish out of water! recording sheet

Draw your fish bowls. Show how much water there is in each one.
Write where you put each one.

This is what I found out:

Name   Date

Annie's tights recording sheet

We are trying to find out

Draw what happened.

I think this happened because

Name   Date

Mr Freeze recording sheet

Draw what you think will happen to each hand.

Draw what you saw when you unwrapped the hands.

This is what I found out:

Mr Freeze goes on holiday

(Based very closely on the Science Challenge Prize-winning play written by Kate Norman and Class 5 of Llantilio Pertholey Primary School, Monmouthshire.)

Characters *(eight characters in total)*
Mr Freeze and Mr Icy *(snowmen)*,
G1 and G2 *(main characters)*,
Child 1, 2, 3 and 4 *(supporting characters)*.

Props
Warm clothes, woolly hat and gloves, summer clothes, sun hat, bucket, carrot, small stones, card carrot 'noses', two postcards, wet towel.

Script

*(The children, G1 and G2 are all on stage, split in to two groups.
Child 1 and 2 are with G1, Child 3 and 4 are with G2.)*

G1 Come on everyone, let's get ready! I'm really looking forward to going on holiday. Two weeks in the boiling hot Hawaii sun, doing absolutely nothing except for soaking up that wonderful heat!

(Snowmen both walk on looking really sad!)

Snowmen What about us? Can't we come too?

Everyone NO!! You'll melt!

G2 We've told you both before: sun, heat and snowmen just don't mix!

G1 Hold on, I've got an idea. Maybe, just maybe! I know! If we dress you properly, I don't see why you can't come with us.

G2 Great idea! I've got a spare sun hat you can borrow, Mr Icy, which should keep you cool! Here you are.

G1 Don't listen to them Mr Freeze, I've got an even better idea! Here's a woolly hat!

(All burst out laughing!)

G2 Sunglasses are what you need, not a woolly hat!

G1 Won't they ever listen! *(Turns to talk to the snowman.)*
Trust us Mr Freeze, what you'll need is a long scarf to wrap up in!

G2 *(Laughing)* We're going to Hawaii, not the North Pole! Don't listen to them. Sun cream is what you'll need – it protects us, so it should protect you too!

G1 Sun cream! Ha! A thick coat is what you'll need. Honest! Trust us! We know what we're talking about!

G2 *(Laughing again)* They must have a screw loose, wrapping a snowman up in all those warm winter clothes! He's going to melt for sure! Here's a pair of summer flip-flops to keep your feet cool!

G1 No! What you need is a thick pair of wellies!

G2 Ha! Wellies! You need a pair of trendy shorts!

G1 Won't they ever learn! Here's a pair of gloves! Right, now, I think we can all go! Come on you lot!

(All sing 'We're all going on a summer holiday' as they leave the stage.)
(Four children come on with two large postcards.)

Child 1 Have you heard from them then?

Child 2 Yes, this arrived this morning. *(Reads from postcard)* 'Having a great time, weather is sooooooo hot! Wish you were here!'

Child 3 What does yours say?

Child 4 'Weather's hot, food's hot, even the babes are hot!' *(With a wiggle)* 'Glad you're not here!' *(Looks sad)*

Child 3 I wish I was!

(G1 returns from holiday laughing and giggling!)

Child 4 Did you have a great time?

G1 Amazing!

Child 1 Where's Mr Freeze? I bet he had a hot time? Ha Ha Ha!

G1 Come on down!

(In walks Mr Freeze with grass skirt and flowers doing the Hula! G2 walks slowly on to the stage looking sad.)

Child 2 What about you? How did you get on?

Child 3 Where's Mr Icy? I bet he had a really cool time!

(In walks G2 with a plastic jar full of water with a carrot, stones and sunglasses in a sun hat on top. Everyone gasps! Oh No!)

G1 We don't like to say we told you so, but we did warn you.

G2 How come Mr Freeze didn't melt in all those winter clothes?

G1 All those thick winter clothes act as thermal insulators! In winter, they stop heat energy getting out, but they also stop heat energy getting in. Basically, they keep hot things hot and cold things cold! Mr Icy hasn't got much of an all-over tan has he!

G2 That's not all of him, that's why. We had a little problem fitting him in the jar. The rest of him is here *(wrings out towel)*. Don't worry, he'll soon evaporate!

G1 What does evaporate mean?

G2 Tune in to next week's adventure as Mr Freeze and Mr Icy travel the world on their water cycle!

All Thank you and goodbye!

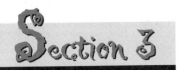

Section 3

This section relates to the Programme of Study: Physical processes (Sc4). Here children begin to develop skills they need to ask questions, observe and explore ideas about the physical world around them. Through practical activities, the basic ideas about phenomena such as light, sound and forces are developed. The use of scientific language, drawings, charts and tables is encouraged to help children communicate their ideas.

SHINE A LIGHT ON ME!

INVESTIGATION TYPE:
FAIR TESTING

RESOURCES AND CLASSROOM ORGANIZATION
A suitable room needs to be found that can be put into complete darkness. If not, perhaps a stock cupboard or even a table covered with a large blanket could be used to create a 'dark' environment. The initial teacher input is to the class as a whole, with the investigation being undertaken by children organized into small groups.
Each group will need:
■ a selection of light sources*
■ a selection of detailed pictures ('Where's Wally?' picture books are ideal for this purpose)
■ measuring tape
■ 'Shine a light on me!' recording sheets – photocopiable page 57.
*Safe sources, such as battery-operated torches, must be used by the children. Other light sources – such as reading lamps, candles and OHPs – can be investigated, but must only be used by the adult in charge, and children must not be left unsupervised with this equipment. The investigation below refers to the use of battery-operated torches.

A great selection of torches can be created if the children are each asked to bring one from home. These can range from normal flashlights to those having coloured and flashing features. It is advisable to check that they all work in advance, and to have spare batteries available. It would be useful to label each torch with a number so that it can be referred to easily.

OBJECTIVES
To give children opportunities to:
■ use information they obtain to develop their scientific ideas
■ explore using their senses
■ make and record simple observations
■ consider the information collected and make simple comparisons
■ try to explain what they have found out.

VOCABULARY
Bright, dark, dim, eyes, light source, see, torch.

BACKGROUND KNOWLEDGE
We see when light is reflected from objects into our eyes. The appearance of the object is affected by the amount of light reflected. In conditions of low light intensity, the details and colour of an object are harder to distinguish. Reflective materials that are used in high-visibility safety clothes have properties that maximize the reflection of light to the viewer.

WHAT TO DO
Discuss with the class how we can see in the dark. Establish the idea that we need light to be able to see. Ask them what objects give us light. They may suggest the Sun, stars, light bulbs, torches, fire, candles and 'glow-in-the-dark' toys. These all produce their own light. The children may also suggest the Moon as a light source,

47

and it is – but it is not producing its own light. We see the Moon because it reflects light from the Sun.

Using the collection of torches, discuss with each group how they might find out which one can be used to see the furthest in the dark. Explain that they are going to test each torch by seeing how far away from the torch they can move a picture and still see the details clearly. Discuss with the group how they can make this investigation a 'fair test'.

To do this, they will need to:

■ make sure the room is dark every time they test

■ make sure the torch stays in the same position

■ move only the picture

■ try to identify the same part of the picture each time

■ measure the distance from the torch to the picture accurately.

Ask the group to make a prediction about which torch they think will work the best, and to give reasons for their choice.

Ask the children to carry out the investigation. For each torch, they should move the picture away until they can no longer clearly see some chosen detail in it. This judgement will need to be a collaborative affair with the whole group agreeing when they can no longer see the picture's details. They should then measure the distance from the torch to the picture and record it on the 'Shine a light on me!' recording sheet (photocopiable page 57).

Once all the torches have been tested, the children can begin to analyse the results. Encourage them to make a simple bar graph showing the distance measured for each torch. The torch with the largest figure is the most effective, and vice versa. Ask the children to give their own reasons for the results. Discuss each group's findings with the class. Allow them to compare their ideas and relate them to their knowledge and understanding of light.

DIFFERENTIATION

More able children could see if there are any other factors that may affect how we see things in dim light; for example, the colour of an object or whether an object is shiny or dull.

Less able children may have difficulty in measuring the distance between the torch and the picture. Instead of using a measuring tape, they could use non-standard units such as hand/foot spans or strips of paper.

SAFETY

Remind children to take care when they are working in low light conditions. They also need to be aware of the risks associated with looking directly at bright lights.

Never allow young children to use candles or light sources powered by mains electricity – adults only must use these.

NOW OR LATER

■ Children could investigate road safety materials such as fluorescent or reflective clothing and safety reflectors. How do these work? Why are they so important?

■ 'Glow-in-the-dark' stars are readily available – the children could investigate how long they will glow for when exposed to light for different periods of time.

■ Ask children to make a list of the many different ways we use light; for example, in traffic lights, flashbulbs and disco lights.

Learn the Ways of the Forces

INVESTIGATION TYPE:
IDENTIFYING AND
CLASSIFYING

Resources and Classroom Organization

Set up an area in the classroom where children can investigate and explore different types of forces in a 'play' environment. Include in this area as many opportunities as you can think of that will provide (or resources that will allow) experiences of different types of force. This activity can easily be adapted to fit into your own classroom themes. Suitable equipment and resources are suggested in the table below.

Resource	Suggested use
Plasticine	for squeezing, twisting, pushing and pulling
soft playdough	for stretching and comparing with the Plasticine, which is harder
wind-up toys	for stopping
various toy cars	for pushing and pulling
string	for pulling
elastic	for stretching
sandpaper and wood	for rubbing
water and objects that will float or sink	for floating and sinking
forcemeters and objects to weigh	for stretching and pulling and weighing objects
various balls	for bouncing and dropping
magnets and steel objects	for observing magnetic forces
'Learn the ways of the forces' recording sheets (photocopiable page 58)	for recording observations

Background Knowledge

Nothing will move unless a force acts upon it. Even when an object is stationary, forces are acting upon it – these forces are balanced. When something is moving at a constant speed in a straight line, the forces acting upon it are equal and opposite, and balanced.

A force is needed to move something, change its shape or direction, or to make it speed up, slow down or stop. The bigger the force, the bigger the effect it has on an object. Gravity is a force that pulls all things towards the centre of the Earth.

Objectives

To give children opportunities to:
■ experience, observe and describe different ways of moving
■ know that pushing or pulling objects can make them start or stop moving
■ find similarities and differences between the movement of different objects.

Vocabulary

Words related to movement: fast, hop, jump, pull, push, slide, slow, spin, swerve, swing, twist, turn. Also: energy, float, force, friction, gravity, sink.

WHAT TO DO

Ask the children *What do you think a force is?* Ask where, and how, they have heard the word 'force' being used. Introduce the children to the 'forces' area of the classroom, and discuss with them all the different objects and materials there. Ask them to explore the different materials and objects. Encourage them to talk about what they are doing, both with you and with each other. Focus their attention on using 'forces' on the objects. Use these conversations to highlight that when we use a force, the object moves or stops or changes shape. Ask the children questions such as those below when referring to different objects:

■ How can I make this car move?

■ What happens if I squeeze this playdough? Will it be different if I poke it with my finger?

■ What happens when I rub this wood with sandpaper? Would it be the same if I rubbed it with ordinary paper?

■ What will happen when these two magnets are pushed together?

■ What will happen when I let go of this ball?

Encourage the children to think of their own questions, which can be recorded by the teacher or by the children themselves, and then to investigate their questions.

Children may use a range of vocabulary to describe their actions. Some may know scientific terms such as 'gravity' and 'friction'. Words such as 'squeeze' or 'pull' can be emphasized with an action, facial expression or intonation. All these actions can reinforce the concept that forces result in some form of action or change in the state of an object.

Children can record their ideas on the 'Learn the ways of the forces' recording sheet (photocopiable page 58). They should 'collect' different types of force and make drawings of their observations on the sheet. Examples of their investigations (a squeezed piece of playdough, for example) can be kept and displayed, along with any questions that the children have suggested.

This activity should be allowed to go on for as long as possible to enable children to take part in both teacher-directed activities and those that are of a 'free play' nature.

DIFFERENTIATION

More able children can be encouraged not only to look at a variety of different forces, but also to be aware of the directions of the forces. For example: *When you push or pull an object, which way does it move?* Children could represent this movement with arrows on their drawings. This can be further developed by looking at the direction in which a force must be applied to stop a moving object.

Less able children might find the free choice of many different objects and different forces distracting. It might be useful, therefore, to introduce them to objects one at a time, and to focus on only one force. For example, children could use just Plasticine to focus on squeezing. Once they have had this experience, they could go on to explore another force.

SAFETY

Remind children that they must be responsible when working together with many different objects. Remind them of the safety issues involved when using objects such as elastic, or when throwing balls. They should remember that forces can do a lot of damage, not just to things in the classroom, but to each other – forces can hurt! It might be a useful exercise to make a list of forces that highlight this. This activity would provide an ideal opportunity to ask children to try to recognize hazards and risks, recording their findings on the 'Keeping it safe!' sheet (photocopiable page 63).

NOW OR LATER

■ The topic of forces can produce some wonderful words. Make a class dictionary of as many words as the children can think of that are associated with forces. Each word could be illustrated with an example of that word. For instance, 'tear' could have a piece of torn paper stuck to the page, 'stretch' could have a piece of elastic attached to the page, and 'squeeze' could be illustrated with something soft to squeeze. This would make the dictionary interactive, and emphasize the properties of each force's action.

■ Use forces to create artwork. This can involve a number of fun, and ultimately messy, methods. For example, children could put blobs of paint onto paper, fold the paper and then use a pushing force to spread the paint out. When they open the paper, they see then pattern they have created. Paint can be applied using other 'force' methods such as blowing with straws, using bubbles, splattering or dripping. The really ambitious could try painting old tennis balls, and then allowing the children to drop, bounce or throw them onto a large sheet of paper – great fun, but very messy! (Best done outside, with lots of overalls.)

■ Ask the children to think up names for the different forces they have discovered. They can use these to create characters, such as Percy Pulling, Penny Push or Magnus Magnetic, for example. Each character could have a description of what it does. Children could act out the role of each character and put together the results into a small play illustrating what they have discovered about forces.

SOUNDS DIFFERENT

INVESTIGATION TYPE:
EXPLORING

RESOURCES AND CLASSROOM ORGANIZATION

This activity is best carried out in small groups and, if possible, in an area where the noise will not disturb others. Before undertaking the investigation, some materials must be wrapped around and secured to beaters.

Each group will need:
■ drums or cymbals
■ a number of beaters
■ a variety of materials to wrap around a beater; for example cotton wool, bubble wrap, silver foil, tissue paper, cling film
■ a variety of objects to use as beaters; for example, spoons, pencils, pieces of spaghetti, feathers, string
■ 'Sounds different' recording sheets – photocopiable page 59
■ tape recorder to record sounds (optional)
■ sound sensor and data-logger (optional).

BACKGROUND KNOWLEDGE

Sounds are created when something vibrates. Actions such as banging, shaking, scraping or plucking strings, and blowing through or over holes in pipes cause vibrations in the surrounding air. Sound travels through the air in waves. The size, shape and frequency of these waves determine the volume, quality and pitch of the sound. Changing the way an object vibrates will change the sound we hear. Sound waves travel through air at a speed of about 344m/s.

WHAT TO DO

Ask the class to sit very still and quiet for a few minutes. In that time, ask them to remember what sounds they can hear. (You can always surprise them with a loud noise at the end to get their attention back.)

Ask questions about the sounds they have heard. Were they loud or quiet? With the class, make lists of loud sounds and quiet sounds.

Demonstrate with the drum how to make a loud sound and how to make a quiet sound. Ask the class how they could make loud and quiet sounds other than by

OBJECTIVES

To give children opportunities to:
■ explore using appropriate senses
■ think about what makes sounds happen
■ make simple comparisons
■ make a record of their observations
■ experience different kinds of sound and sources of sound.

VOCABULARY

Words that describe sounds: hard, high, loud, low, muffled, quiet, soft.

varying they way they hit the drum. If needed, direct them to the idea of changing the beater, and changing what the beater is made of, in particular.

Divide the class into small groups. Explain that they are going to test some different beaters to see if they make loud or quiet sounds. Show the children the range of beaters, and describe the materials that they are made of. Discuss with the children the properties of the materials. Ask them to predict which one will make the quietest sound and which the loudest, and to record their ideas on the 'Sounds different' recording sheet (photocopiable page 59). They should decide on some sort of order, from the beater they think will make the quietest sound to the one that will make the loudest. Ask each child in turn to describe reasons for their choices.

Next, the children should carry out the test. They should hit the drum with each beater in turn. Ask them to compare the noise levels created by each beater, and to place the beaters in order. They can repeat this process until the whole group is happy with the order. The group can then record their findings on the 'Sounds different' recording sheet. Encourage the children to compare their results with their initial guesses, and discuss with them the similarities and differences between the two lists. Ask the children to think about why some beaters made louder noises than others.

A tape recorder can be used to record the sounds made. When playing back the tape, they can get some idea of how loud the sound is by using the volume control; they can turn down the volume until they can only just hear the sound, and use the number on the dial as an indication of 'loudness' (the smaller the number, the louder the sound).

Using a sound sensor and data-logger provides a more accurate indication of the loudness of the sounds, which may be represented by values in decibels or as a graph. This approach provides an excellent way of working with sounds with children, as they are able to see real values from which they can make better judgements in their science work.

NOW OR LATER

■ Children could make a 'sound diary', in which they record the sounds they hear throughout the day, explain what the sounds are, and say whether they like each sound or not.

■ Children could make 'sound journeys' using tape recorders: they plan a journey around the school, recording the sounds encountered on the way.

■ Using a simple computer program such as 'sound recorder' (found in Windows) and a microphone, children can to record their own voice and see the sound vibrations it makes. The can also see how these vibrations change when they make louder sounds.

FLOAT AWAY!

INVESTIGATION TYPE:
FAIR TESTING

RESOURCES AND CLASSROOM ORGANIZATION

Before undertaking this investigation, children should have experience of exploring materials to see which float and which sink.

This activity is best undertaken by children in small groups. Since water is to be used, choose a work area where spills and puddles will not damage the floor or surroundings. The bottle 'boats' must be prepared beforehand by an adult: in order to avoid having to use a large number of marbles, first place the bottle on its side in water, and mark the water level; then cut the side of the boat down to about 1cm above this mark.

Each group will need:
■ washing-up bowl or water tray
■ three empty plastic pop bottles of varying sizes (eg 100ml, 500ml, 1 litre) made into 'boats' (see above)
■ marbles (or anything that is small and will provide enough weight)
■ 'Float away!' recording sheets – photocopiable page 60.

BACKGROUND KNOWLEDGE

Buoyancy (or upthrust) is the upward force on an object immersed in a fluid. If the upward force is greater than the downward force of gravity on the object (its weight), the object will float. If the weight is greater than the buoyancy, it will sink.

There are two main factors that decide whether an object floats or not. The first is its density. For example, a ping pong ball will float in water because it has a low density, while a golf ball will sink (higher density). The second factor affecting whether or not an object will float in water is its shape. For example, a ball of Plasticine will sink, but if the same ball is flattened out into a hollow cup shape and placed on the surface it will float. The buoyancy is equal to the weight of water displaced by the object, so if the object displaces more water, the buoyancy is greater. The ball of Plasticine displaces a much smaller volume of water than the cup shape, so the buoyancy of the ball is smaller than that of the cup – the ball sinks, but the cup floats. Another way of thinking about it, which is perhaps easier for children, is that the water pushes up on an object in the opposite direction to gravity, which is pulling the object down. The larger the area of an object that the water can push against, the greater the upthrust is, so the more likely it is that the object will float (provided that its weight is not so large as to outweigh the upthrust).

WHAT TO DO

Discuss with the children the three bottle 'boats'. Ask them which one they think could hold the most marbles before it sinks. Highlight to the class that as they add marbles, the boat will become heavier – do they think this might make a difference? Explain that they are going to test each boat in turn. To do this they must make the test fair. Ask for their suggestions of how to make it a fair test. They might suggest:
■ using the same sized marbles for each boat
■ placing the marbles in carefully

OBJECTIVES
To give children opportunities to:
■ develop their own scientific ideas
■ use drawings to present scientific information
■ suggest what might happen in an investigation
■ recognize that a comparison may not always be fair
■ make simple comparisons.

VOCABULARY
Bottle, float, force, marbles, push, pull, sink, water.

cut out this section

plastic pop bottle (with lid)

■ making sure there is no water in the boats
■ making sure they count correctly.

These suggestions could be written down and displayed, to remind children of them during the activity.

In their groups, ask the children to have a guess at how many marbles each boat will hold before it sinks. Ask them to give possible reasons for their guesses.

Now the children should carry out the investigation, testing each boat in turn and following the rules they decided on earlier to make it a fair test. Encourage each group to repeat each test so that they can check their findings, and remind them to stick to the fair test rules each time.

Once the children have completed the investigation, ask them to record their results on the 'Float away!' recording sheet (photocopiable page 60). They should draw each boat with a representation of how many marbles were used to sink it.

Once the whole class has completed the investigation, discuss the results and ask for possible reasons for them. They should have found that the larger boat is able to hold more marbles. From the discussion, highlight the idea that the water has more to push up against with the larger boat, so the force holding the boat up is bigger. This means that the boat can hold more weight.

When asking the children to draw their observations, direct them to look closely at the way the boat is actually sitting in the water. It will not be floating flat on the surface, but will have sunk down a little (it has pushed away some water).

SAFETY

Remind children of the importance of working sensibly, carefully and responsibly, especially as they are working with water: spilling the water would not only cause a mess, but it could also make the floor dangerously slippery.

DIFFERENTIATION

More able children could produce a simple bar graph of their results, or investigate how flattening a ball of Plasticine can make a boat that can hold marbles.

Less able children might try to push the three bottle boats down with their fingers, rather than using marbles, so that they can feel which one is harder to sink.

NOW OR LATER

■ Children could collect a range of different plastic bottles and test them to see which one would make the best boat to hold the most marbles.
■ Children could make boats out of junk – but they must float!
■ Visit the nearest swimming pool so that the children can experience floating for themselves, and see how changing their shape in the water affects the way they float.

ON AND OFF, OFF AND ON

INVESTIGATION TYPE:
EXPLORING; IDENTIFYING AND CLASSIFYING

OBJECTIVES

To give children opportunities to:
■ ask questions about their ideas in science
■ think about what is expected to happen
■ make simple comparisons and observations
■ try to explain what they have found out
■ explore circuits.

RESOURCES AND CLASSROOM ORGANIZATION

Young children may have difficulty in handling electrical components and connecting them together. This can make this type of investigation problematic. Many of these problems can be overcome by purchasing a kit that is specifically designed for children at KS1. Alternatively, a homemade method of securing the components and simple ways of connecting them can be used, as shown opposite.

The class will need:
■ a range of electrical components (3.5V bulbs, bulb holders, 1.5V batteries, battery holders, switches, buzzers)
■ small pieces of wooden board upon which to attach the components to make circuits
■ crocodile clips with wire leads
■ Velcro

- plastic tape
- 'On and off, off and on' recording sheets 1 and 2 – photocopiable pages 61 and 62
- materials to test: for example, chalk, paper clips, paper, pencils, rubber, metal and non-metal objects.

VOCABULARY

Words relating to electrical circuits: battery, bulb, bulb holder, buzzer, circuit, connection, crocodile clip, mains, switch, wire.

Section 3

BACKGROUND KNOWLEDGE

An electric current is a flow of particles called electrons through a material. For the components in a circuit, such as bulbs or buzzers to work, the circuit must be complete. Breaking the circuit will stop the flow of electrical current and the components will not work. One device used to control the flow of current is called a switch. Materials such as metals allow current to flow through them fairly easily. They can be described as electrical conductors. Materials that do not allow current to flow easily are described as electrical insulators.

WHAT TO DO

Before undertaking this investigation, make sure that all the electrical components are working and that the batteries have sufficient charge. Discuss with the children their ideas about electricity and its uses. Remind them of the dangers of electricity, particularly of mains electricity. These ideas should be considered in activities about safety and electricity in the home, undertaken before carrying out this investigation.

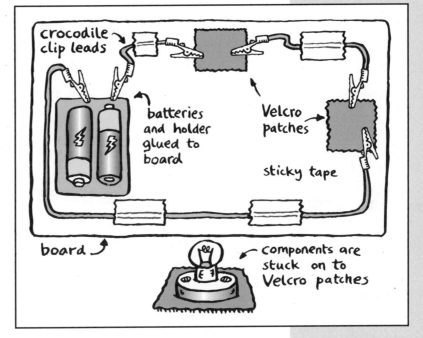

The children can carry out this investigation in small groups. – this reduces the amount of equipment needed. Show the children in each group the different electrical components. Ask them what they think each is called, what it does and how it works. The group could record their ideas in words and/or pictures, which will give the teacher an opportunity to make sure that each child at least understands the name of each component.

Provide each group with a 'circuit board' set up as shown above, plus a bulb in a bulb holder and an additional crocodile clip lead. Ask the children how they could make the bulb work – they need to connect up the bulb and the extra lead to make a complete circuit. Allow the children to work this out by trial and improvement. If they haven't managed to make a working circuit after a suitable time period, then offer help and guide them through the activity. Ask them to draw the circuit they have made, and label the components on 'On and off, off and on' recording sheet 1 (photocopiable page 61). Also ask the children to describe how they think the circuit works (though it is not important that they describe an electrical current in accurate terms at this stage). Ask questions such as those below:

- Is the bulb on or off?
- How can we make the bulb go on and then off?
- What happens when we swap the positions of the components?
- Can we try different types of components; two bulbs, for example, or a buzzer instead of the bulb?
- What happens when we disconnect a lead?

From this activity, the children should understand the idea that an electrical component must be in a complete circuit for it to work.

Allow the groups some time to freely explore their circuits, and ask them to record their discoveries on recording sheet 1.

Ask the children to build a circuit with a bulb and two crocodile leads (see the diagram below). These leads must have free ends. Test the circuit by touching the free ends together, then give each group a number of familiar objects made from different materials (some should be metal and some non-metal). Ask the children which materials they think will make the bulb go on, and which will not. Ask them to record their ideas on recording sheet 2 (photocopiable page 62), then allow them to test the materials and sort them into two groups: those that make the bulb go on, and those that do not. Ask the children to compare their original predictions with their results. What do they notice about the materials that made the bulb go on?

From this activity, the children should understand that metals can complete the circuit, and are used to make electrical components.

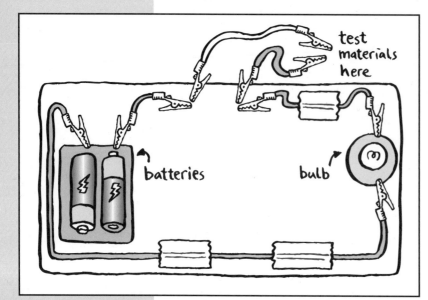

test materials here

batteries

bulb

DIFFERENTIATION

Most children can cope with making circuits – it is often only the complexity of the kit or equipment they are using that hinders them. If some children do not have the co-ordination to connect up the circuit, make the circuit for them beforehand.

More able children could build more complicated circuits involving more than one component.

SAFETY

Remind children of the dangers of electricity, especially mains electricity. Make children aware of the glass bulbs and how to act responsibly when handling them. Placing the bulbs in bulb holders beforehand makes them easier for children to handle. Do not allow children to connect a complete circuit with just a battery; this will cause a short circuit, resulting in the wires and battery becoming very hot. If in doubt, consult your school's safety policy or the ASE publication 'Be Safe' (ISBN 0 86357 081 X).

NOW OR LATER

■ Children could make a poster giving advice about the dangers of electricity.
■ Children could make simple models (of a house or car, for example) and make a simple circuit to put a light inside.
■ Children could try their hand at this 'Game of skill':
Bend a wire coat hanger into a wobbly shape and fix it firmly to a piece of wood. Make a loop around the coat hanger wire out of stiff wire. Make a simple circuit using a buzzer and bulb as shown below. Connect one lead to the coat hanger, and the other to the wire loop. The children have to move the loop along the coat hanger without touching it, otherwise the buzzer will sound.

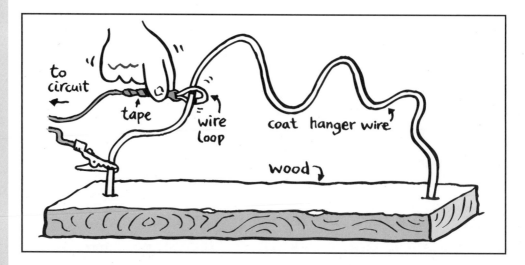

to circuit

tape

wire loop

coat hanger wire

wood

Shine a light on me! recording sheet

How I made this investigation a 'fair test':

Torch number	Distance of picture

I found out that

Name _____   Date _____

Learn the ways of the forces recording sheet

When I use a force, I can make something _____.

When I use a force, I can change the _____ of something.

Pushing force	Pulling force
Rubbing force	Spinning force
_____ force	_____ force

Sounds different recording sheet

I think this will happen:

This is what I found out:

▼ Loud ▼	▼ Loud ▼
▲ Quiet ▲	▲ Quiet ▲

Ready to go! IDEAS FOR SCIENCE INVESTIGATIONS

Name _____   Date _____

Float away! recording sheet

On and off, off and on recording sheet 1

Draw the circuits
you have made.

This is a complete circuit.

I made this circuit by myself.

On and off, off and on recording sheet 2

Test the things you have been given. Do they make the light go on, or does it stay off? Decide which group each one should go in.

Things that
make the light go on

Things that don't
make the light go on

Keeping it safe!

Whenever we do a science investigation we must think about safety. It is very important that whatever we work with, we must do it safely.

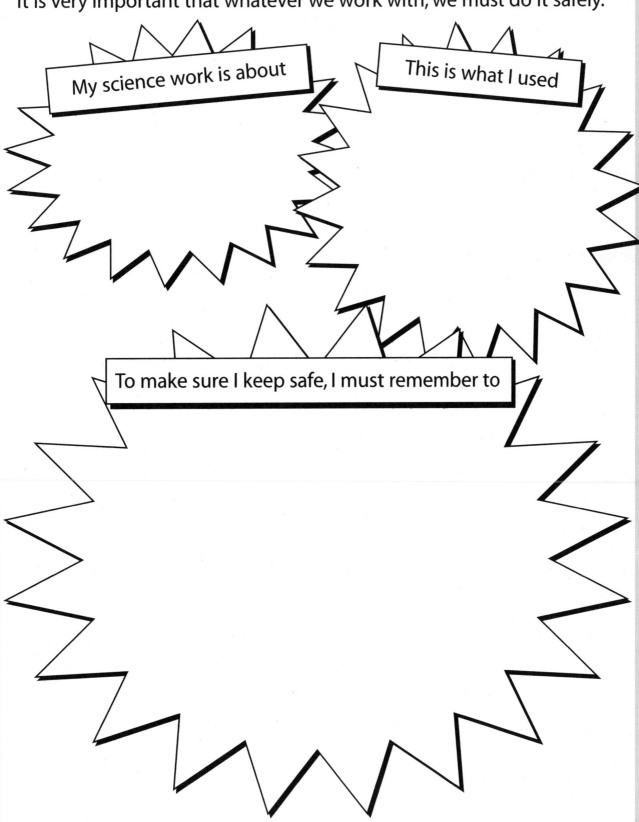

My science work is about

This is what I used

To make sure I keep safe, I must remember to

NATIONAL STANDARDS FOR KEY SKILLS

Skills Grid

SKILLS (☑ = elements of the skill are introduced) Children have opportunities to…

Skill groupings:
- IDEAS AND EVIDENCE IN SCIENCE
- INVESTIGATIVE SKILLS – PLANNING
- INVESTIGATIVE SKILLS – OBTAINING AND PRESENTING EVIDENCE
- INVESTIGATIVE SKILLS – CONSIDERING EVIDENCE AND EVALUATING

Activity	Investigation Type	Collect evidence to try to answer a question	Ask questions and decide how they might find answers to them	Use first-hand experience and simple information sources to answer questions	Think about what might happen before deciding what to do	Recognize when a test or comparison is unfair	Follow simple instructions to control the risks to themselves and to others	Explore using appropriate senses, and make and record observations and measurements	Communicate what happened in a variety of ways, including using ICT	Make simple comparisons and identify simple patterns or associations	Compare what happened with any predictions made; draw upon their knowledge and understanding to try to offer an explanation	Review their work and explain to others what they did	QCA Ref. Unit	National Curriculum references
HANDY HANDS	Pattern seeking	✓	✓	✓	✓	☑	✓	✓	✓	✓	✓	✓	1A	Sc2 2a/4a
PLANTS AND LIGHT	Exploring	✓	✓	✓		☑		✓	✓	✓	✓	✓	1B	Sc2 3a/3c
SAY IT WITH FLOWERS	Investigating models; Identifying and classifying	✓	✓	✓	✓	✓	✓	✓	✓	✓		✓	2C	Sc2 3b/4b
PHEW! WHY AM I OUT OF BREATH?	Fair testing	✓	✓	✓		☑	✓	✓	✓	✓	☑	✓	2A	Sc2 2c
SNACK ATTACK!	Pattern seeking	✓	✓	✓		✓		✓		✓	☑	✓	2B	Sc2 2b
SKIPPING TEST	Exploring	✓	✓	✓		☑		✓	✓	✓	✓	✓	2D	Sc3 1a/b/c/d 2a
OH DEAR! MOP IT UP!	Fair testing	✓	✓	✓		☑		✓		✓		✓	2D	Sc3 1a/b
STICKY STUFF	Pattern seeking	✓	✓	✓	✓	✓	✓	✓	✓	✓	✓	✓	1C/2D	Sc3 1a/2a
BUBBLES!	Exploring	✓	✓	✓			✓	✓	✓	✓		✓	2D	Sc3 1a/b
A FISH OUT OF WATER!	Pattern seeking	✓	✓	✓		✓	✓	✓	✓	✓	✓	✓	2D	Sc3 2b
ANNIE'S TIGHTS	Fair testing	✓	✓	✓		☑	✓	✓	✓	✓	✓	✓	2E	Sc3 2b
MR FREEZE	Pattern seeking	✓	✓	✓		✓	✓	✓	✓	✓		✓	2D	Sc3 2b
SHINE A LIGHT ON ME!	Fair testing	✓	✓	✓	✓	☑	✓	✓	✓	✓	✓	✓	1D	Sc4 3a/b
LEARN THE WAYS OF THE FORCES	Identifying and classifying	✓	✓	✓			✓	✓	✓	✓	✓	✓	2E	Sc4 2a/b/c
SOUNDS DIFFERENT	Exploring	✓	✓	✓				✓	✓	✓	✓	✓	1F	Sc4 3c/d
FLOAT AWAY!	Fair testing	✓	✓	✓	✓	✓		✓	✓	✓	✓	✓	1E/2E	Sc4 2a/b
ON AND OFF, OFF AND ON	Exploring; Identifying and classifying	✓	✓	✓	✓	✓	✓	✓	✓	✓	✓	✓	2F	Sc4 1a/b/c